Your Most Complete Astrological Guide to Timing Love Relationships

For all of you who have wandered or rushed blindly into inappropriate, unfulfilling, or disastrous marriages, don't blame yourself. Blame a lack of astrological know-how—the kind that you will learn from this book! Before you say "I do," whether it's for the first time or the fifth, check the odds first with the proven methods explained in these pages.

When Will You Marry? shows everyone—from astrological novices to advanced students—how to use this premier technique to find out when love is likely in your life. Instruction progresses from the basics—such as compatible elements and Sun signs—to the finer points of romantic indicators such as Sun/Moon midpoints, chart link-ups, and Arabian Parts. And observations on the charts of famous couples, from Marie Antoinette and Louis XVI to Joanne Woodward and Paul Newman, will show you how the "love planets" can make or break your relationships!

Whether you're 18 or 80, whom to look for and when is a vital question. And *When Will You Marry?* has the answer! The methods explained in this book are the result of years of research into what astrology has to say about timing and the success or failure of romantic relationships. Know for certain whether that wonderful person you've just met (or the one in your future) is *meant* to be a part of your life—and when your dreams of a happy marriage will come true.

About the Author

As a columnist for *Dell Horoscope Magazine* ("Astro-Quiz"), an author of numerous articles for popular astrology publications, a counselor and lecturer, and a teacher of advanced astrology at the Carroll Righter Foundation in Hollywood, Rose Murray has had much experience in reaching a wide variety of individuals interested in astrology and what it can do for them.

As a helpful, happily-married Virgo, with home-loving Cancer rising and Moon in Cancer, Rose would like to aid everyone in finding a perfect mate. With her Mars conjunct Mercury in romantic Libra, she realizes how vital a loving relationship can be to happiness. And with Jupiter in compassionate Pisces conjunct Uranus in pioneering Aries in her tenth house of career, she's always looking for innovative ways to help people fulfill their lives.

To Write to the Author

If you wish to contact the author, please write to her in care of Llewellyn Worldwide, and we will forward your request. Both the author and the publisher appreciate hearing from you and learning of your enjoyment of this book and how it has helped you. Llewellyn Worldwide cannot guarantee that every letter written to the author can be answered, but all will be forwarded. Please write to:

Rose Murray
c/o Llewellyn Worldwide
P.O. Box 64383-K479-0, St. Paul, MN 55164-0383, U.S.A.

Please enclose a self-addressed, stamped envelope or $1.00 to cover costs.
If outside the U.S.A., enclose international postal reply coupon.

Free Catalog from Llewellyn

For more than 90 years Llewellyn has brought its readers knowledge in the fields of metaphysics and human potential. Learn about the newest books in spiritual guidance, natural healing, astrology, occult philosophy and more. Enjoy book reviews, new age articles, a calendar of events, plus current advertised products and services. To get your free copy of *Llewellyn's New Worlds of Mind and Spirit*, send your name and address to:

Llewellyn's New Worlds of Mind and Spirit
P.O. Box 64383-K479-0, St. Paul, MN 55164-0383, U.S.A.

Llewellyn's Popular Astrology Series

When Will You Marry?

Your Romantic Destiny Through Astrology

Rose Murray

1995
Llewellyn Publications
St. Paul, Minnesota, U.S.A. 55164-0383

FIRST EDITION
First Printing, 1995

Cover design: Lynne Menturweck
Cover painting: Martin Skoro
Book design, layout, and editing: Susan Van Sant

Library of Congress Cataloging-in-Publication Data
Murray, Rose, 1927–
    When will you marry? : your romantic destiny through astrology /
Rose Murray. — 1st ed.
       p.   cm.
    Includes bibliographical references and index.
    ISBN 1-56718-479-0 (softbound : alk. paper)
    1. Astrology and marriage.   2. Mate selection — Miscellanea.
3. Celebrities — Miscellanea. I. Title.
BF1729.L6M87   1995
133.5'864677 — dc20   95-2101
                                                              CIP

Llewellyn Publications
A Division of Llewellyn Worldwide, Ltd.
P.O. 64383, St. Paul, MN 55164-0383

About Llewellyn's Popular Astrology Series

Astrology has been called "the oldest science," for it has evolved from humanity's first sense of wonder at the Universe round about, and from humanity's earliest efforts at finding meaning to their place in the Universe.

Astrology sees the Universe as "organic"—alive and interrelated at every level and place. Astrology sees an individual as a miniature of the Universe—the Microcosm to the Macrocosm—and ascribes to the Hermetic axiom: As Above, So Below. Astrology sees the movements of the planets within the solar system in which we live as having meaningful relationship to events on Earth and in the lives of humanity. Based on that concept, astrology may be used to gain better understanding of those events on Earth and in people's lives, and to forecast trends based on the cyclical movements of the planets.

Llewellyn is the oldest astrological organization in the Western Hemisphere, and has always sought to bring to the public the practical benefits of applied astrology. In this series of Popular Astrology books, we bring to the layperson text without involvement in complex calculations or difficult terminology, intended to give the reader the opportunity to—in some sense—take command over his or her life by understanding the planetary factors at work.

Our world is complex, and each of us lives at the vortex of a flow of mighty forces. But each of us can, with knowledge, reach out in conscious interrelationship to the planetary factors and give positive direction to the play of forces to reflect better our hopes and ideals.

We can shape our destiny! We cannot only live our lives better, but we can and must assume more responsibility for the greater community in which we live and have our being. Humanity today has too much power, and too little; it is only with awareness of the trends in current events that we can take responsible action to resolve the many challenges of the next few years. Astrology, and this book in particular, brings this awareness to everyone.

Popular Astrology gives people insight into human nature and into Nature itself. With vision, there is the power to take action. To act with awareness of trends is to assume responsibility. And to act responsibly is the mark of an awakened human being.

Carl Llewellyn Weschcke

Other Books by Rose Murray

Astro-Numerology: A New Look at An Ancient Mystic Art. A.F.A., 1991.

The Love Book: Creative Methods to Attract Your Ideal Mate. RMM Publishing, 1981 and 1985.

Marilyn: The Last Months. Pyramid Press, N.Y., 1975.

Acknowledgements

I wish to thank my husband, Norman Edward Wilson, for his Jupiter-on-my-Sun-in-my-third-house-of-writing encouragement and for having a chart that goes so well with mine (again this lifetime); my daughter, Diannah Morgan, for her Uranian-grand-trine technological expertise that has kept my computer up and running; my brother, Victor Murray, for lending his Mercury-in-Scorpio eagle-eye to help catch errors; my lovely Pisces Aunt Helen, whose fondness for the mysteries of life has been a guiding light; all my astrological colleagues who've been helpful, especially Jack Taube, whose Jupiter-conjunct-Uranus-in-his-house-of-friends has always made astrology more fun; and, of course, to Susan Van Sant at Llewellyn, for her Virgo-Sun-Cancer-Moon expertise and talents that have made this book as beautiful as it is.

Table of Contents

Table of Illustrations and Diagrams x

Preface: How To Predict Your Own Marriage xi

1. The Compatibility Secrets of the Ancients: The Love Planets 1

2. When the Love Planets Are Most Likely to Attract Partners
to Members of Your Sun Sign............................. 15

3. What You Need In a Marriage Partner 33

4. When The Planets Overhead Make Lucky Aspects to
Your Natal Love Planets: The Transits 47

5. A Compatibility Checkup With Someone You've Met 61

6. Determining Mutual Money Luck 81

7. When Your Progressed Planets Promise Love or Marriage........... 95

8. Love Links Between Charts at the Time of Marriage................ 113

9. The Sun/Moon Midpoint as a Marriage Indicator and Timer........ 121

10. Arabic Parts and Karmic Ties.................................... 133

Appendix A: Chart Services 151

Appendix B: Chart Sources.............................. 153

Appendix C: Celebrity Charts 155

Glossary.. 188

Bibliography 198

Index... 200

Table of Illustrations and Diagrams

Where to Find Marriage and Romance in a Chart 36

Decanates 45

Duads 45

Power Points — The Four Angles in a Chart 60

Favorable or Challenging Conjunctions 74

Finding Marriage Years in the Natal Chart:
    A. Counting Degrees Between Love Planets and Angles 98
    B. Counting Degrees Between Part of Marriage
       and Love Planets (Angle) 99
    C. Dividing Distance by Half Between Planets and
       Angles Approaching Each Other — One by
       Progression, One by Converse 100

Finding Marriage Years in the Ephemeris 102

360 Degree Conversion Table 124

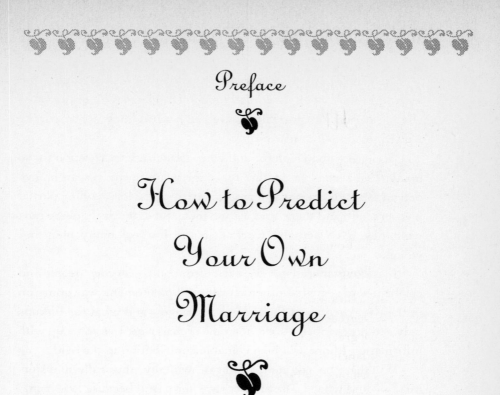

How to Predict Your Own Marriage

"Do you see marriage for me this year?" is a question I hear frequently as a professional astrologer. Everyone wants to know the answer—from teen-agers to those advanced in age. Marriage is still an almost-universal hope and dream for most single, divorced, or widowed individuals.

Of course, my clients also phone me from time to time with another urgent request: "I've just met someone—and I need to know if this one is right for me!"

This book has the answers—to both queries—answers that can help you know when it's a good time to circulate and meet as many eligible persons as possible, as well as how to know when Mr. or Ms. Right actually turns up.

Because who to look for and when is such a vital question for so many, I've zeroed in on this topic for years in my research. I've delved through ancient and modern astrological lore, culling partial answers here and there, and testing them out extensively to see how well they have actually worked in the lives of many men and women.

I've also gathered marriage data from both everyday people and celebrities to see what other astrological phenomena was going on in their horoscopes at the time of marriage—and what the linkups between horoscopes were at the time of marriage. I've come up with information I hope will be a valuable contribution to the field.

Will there be true compatibility—mentally, physically, and spiritually—and when? The answers are here. And because love sometimes flies out the window when financial hardships are too great, I've also researched and included information on how you can astrologically assure a mutually satisfactory financial situation in your marriage.

Who is right for you in love and marriage has been treated in publications often. Many books have been written on astrological compatibility, from simple guides that tell you the best signs for you, to advanced methods of chart comparison that go more deeply into the subject.

But up until this book, no one has focused on the equally important subject of *when you will marry*, nor on the uncanny linkups between charts, Arabian parts, Sun/Moon midpoints, and other fine points that I use in this book.

If you've been interested in astrology for a while, you probably already have a copy of your natal chart, and may know a trine from a sextile, a house from a cusp, or which signs go best with yours. If you've missed out on any such basic information, however, what you need to know to use my method will be explained in easy steps, chapter by chapter.

By the time you get to the later chapters of the books, you'll find methods of fine-tuning compatibility and marriage timing that will confirm with great exactness whether a particular person was meant to be in your life—and when marriage is most likely.

A friend told me recently that when she met the man she was later to marry her professional-astrologer-mother told her: "Marry him—this will be a long-lasting union—and you'll never want for anything financially." It all turned out to be true.

If one of my parents had been an astrologer (or had access to a book like this), they might have seen that my first marriage would be a disaster.

Instead, without the wisdom of the stars, my practical Virgo father, who had only a few months to live and was worried about my welfare when he was gone, told me: "Marry H—he's the type who will take good care of you."

My father turned out to be 100% wrong; five years later Mr. Wrong and I parted because of his irresponsibility. An astrological chart would have revealed the true story.

For all of you who've wandered—or rushed—blindly into disastrous, inappropriate, or unfulfilling marriages, don't blame yourself, your parents, or your judgment. Blame a lack of the kind of astrological knowledge that you can learn in this book.

And for all of you who've yet to take the plunge—or want to try again—with the information in these pages, you can smile all the way to the altar.

Not only will this book show you when it's a good time to circulate and meet as many eligible persons as possible, but how to determine whether love, happiness, and security lie ahead with a particular individual.

Even if you read no more than the first chapter, you'll have more information than I did when I walked down the aisle and into the arms of the wrong man so long ago.

For all who read this book, may you be enriched by the methods I've discovered to find out more about your love life.

Rose Murray
Santa Monica, CA
1993

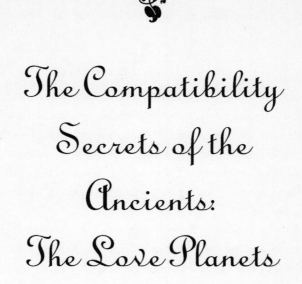

Chapter One

The Compatibility
Secrets of the
Ancients:
The Love Planets

What special chemistry draws you to one person and not another? Why do some love affairs and marriages succeed while others fail? Poets and songwriters, psychologists and philosophers have pondered such questions over the years.

Astrologers have known the answers for centuries. As far back as the second century A.D., the greatest figure in ancient astrology, Ptolemy, wrote down the magic formula for a happy marriage in his *Tetrabiblos*.

The answer lies in the harmony of Sun, Moon, Venus, and Mars in the horoscopes of potential lovers. For a real attraction, the kind that endures, certain patterns must exist between the two charts. Many heartaches and broken marriages might be spared if more persons knew and used the rules of basic astrological compatibility.

The Formula

The tie between the two Suns should promise harmony, first of all, for friendliness and compatible temperaments to exist. Then a good Sun/Moon tie would promise the appreciation of each other's male or female qualities that is needed in marriage. For sexual attraction, a good Venus/Mars tie between the two charts would indicate that physical passion would be strong enough to endure. That is the basic formula.

In my research over the years, I have almost always found these rules to be valid. When one of the factors is missing, a substitute aspect may sometimes suffice. More often, the marriage doesn't occur, is terribly frustrating, stormy, or otherwise difficult to sustain. The complete formula is described in more detail in Chapter Five, "A Compatibility Checkup with Someone You've Met."

Sun Sign Compatibility

First, and possibly most important, is that instant harmony occurs between two people whose Suns are in compatible signs (see page 3). There immediately arises a kind of understanding and easy camaraderie with such persons that makes getting along easier than with others.

If the aspect is close to exact, there is even more harmony. There are thirty degrees in each sign, and if both are born in a similar or close degree, the harmony is even stronger. Thus Clark Gable, born near 12 degrees of Aquarius, and Carole Lombard, born near 13 degrees of the compatible sign, Libra, felt great rapport for each other.

All kinds of partnerships benefit through this Sun/Sun link-up. Even in the movies, the most popular love teams of Hollywood's golden years in the 30s and 40s were invariably astrologically well-matched. Whether the studios employed an astrologer behind the scenes to make these money-making matches, or whether they occurred naturally, I don't know.

Garbo and Gilbert, Astaire and Rogers, Myrna Loy and William Powell, Taylor and Burton were just some of the famous pairs whose horoscopes together created the rapport that led to public interest and box office success.

In the book, *Hollywood's Great Love Teams*, written by James Robert Parish (New Rochelle, N.Y.: Arlington House Publishers, 1974), twenty-eight well-known love teams of Hollywood's golden years were featured. Parish included birth data and Sun sign information on each star. Only a few of the pairs were not compatible by Sun sign.

Sun Sign Compatibility is Elemental

It's easiest to discover and remember those signs compatible with yours if you relate each sign of the zodiac to its element, either Fire, Earth, Air, or Water.

The Fire Signs — Aries, Leo, and Sagittarius are fiery, high-spirited and active. They are compatible with each other and with the Air signs—Gemini, Libra, and Aquarius.

The Earth Signs — Taurus, Virgo, and Capricorn are practical, down-to-earth, traditional. They are compatible with each other and with the Water signs—Cancer, Scorpio, and Pisces.

The Air Signs — Gemini, Libra, and Aquarius are objective, intellectual, and highly sociable. They are compatible with each other and with the Fire signs—Aries, Leo, and Sagittarius.

The Water Signs — Cancer, Scorpio, and Pisces are emotional, receptive, and inner-directed. They are compatible with each other and with the Earth signs—Taurus, Virgo, and Capricorn.

The differences are a matter of temperament. Generally speaking, the Fire and Air signs tend to be more active and volatile. Earth and Water tend to be quieter and more subdued.

An Interesting Experiment

The most graphic and dramatic example I've seen of these differences occurred at a singles party where I was giving a talk about astrology. As an experiment, I asked the Fire and Air sign people to withdraw to one side of the room. I asked the Earth and Water signs to take the other side. I was going to do some instant matchmaking.

Each group was then to await further instructions, but the Fire and Air signs, once out of their chairs, would not settle down again. Their side of the room became ablaze with fire-and-air-swept circulating, socializing, flirting, and loud talk. It was quite difficult to gain their attention again for the next step of the experiment.

The Earth and Water signs, however, took their new seats promptly, waiting politely for further instructions.

You Gain From Compatible Elements

You draw vitality from persons of compatible elements, while a member of an incompatible Sun sign can actually drain you of energy. This is especially true if you're in contact too long. Steven Arroyo, in his fascinating book, *Astrology and the Four Elements,* has pointed this out. He suggested that if two people of incompatible elements are married, they should not share the same bed for long hours at night.

Aspects Between Signs and the Love Planets

If you're not familiar with the astrological term "aspects," you should know that signs or planets which are trine (120 degrees) or sextile (60 degrees) to each other are harmonious. They're always compatible by element.

Oppositions (180 degrees) are also compatible by element, but may be more difficult to blend. When Sun is opposite Sun, or Sun opposite Moon, bringing together the opposite traits involved may not be difficult, but when Venus is opposite Mars, there is usually much more potential for conflict.

An example of Sun opposite Sun can be found in the charts of Aquarian Burt Reynolds and Leo Loni Anderson. In this case, opposites did attract, but the potential for conflict finally came out and they went their separate ways.

Squares (90 degrees) sometimes attract quite energetically, but the difference of element involved usually spells trouble, no matter what the love planets involved. One sees this attraction quite often between the fixed-sign squares (Taurus and Leo, Taurus and Aquarius, Leo and Scorpio, or Scorpio and Aquarius). These strong and stubborn individuals are often attracted to other strong and stubborn individuals like themselves who pose a challenge to them. If the marriage lasts, it's often because fixed signs rarely like to admit defeat.

Famous couples who have married despite Sun square Sun include President Bill Clinton, a Leo, and Hillary Rodham Clinton, a Scorpio. The Scorpio/Leo combination is also seen in the marriage of Leo Arnold Schwarzenegger and Scorpio Maria Shriver.

Fire Sign Romances

The Fire signs—Aries, Leo, and Sagittarius—seem most fulfilled and in their element when teamed with other members of these signs or with the Air signs—Gemini, Libra, and Aquarius. Sometimes members of the same sign don't get along well if they are too much alike. Two Leos, for example, might compete for the limelight. Two Leos who did hit it off, at least on the silver screen, were William Powell and Myrna Loy. They co-starred in early-day Hollywood's *Thin Man* series of movies.

Generally, two members of the same sign will get along very well—or not at all. Madonna and Sean Penn, both Leos, were married in August, 1985, but didn't stay together. They may have found too many similarities to contend with. Kathie Lee and Frank Gifford, on the other hand, also both Leos, married on October 18, 1986, and remain together as of this writing.

Fire sign individuals are usually happiest when paired with other Fire-sign natives. Melanie Griffith, a Leo, and Don Johnson, a Sagittarian, are a good example. Whether they stay together or not, they are well matched astrologically. Their Suns are trine each other. They have good Sun/Moon ties by sign, and a great Venus/Mars conjunction between charts.

Fire and Air is often a good combination. John Fitzgerald Kennedy, a Gemini, chose Jacqueline Bouvier, a fiery Leo, with an Aries Moon, for his bride. Her fire-sign vivacity sometimes stole the show, even from someone with his Gemini wit and sociability. Adding to this Sun sign tie was a strong Venus-to-Venus tie, which indicated they would delight in the same type of social fun and splendor, some of which lent their White House years the flavor of a modern-day Camelot.

Jackie also had a strong Mars trine Mars tie with JFK, which showed they could cooperate in practical endeavors. Even this was not a perfect union in the sense that Ptolemy advocated, however.

6

There was no tie between Venus and Mars for physical passion, except a disharmonious square aspect.

A Moon/Mars exchange, however, did make up for this somewhat. If he strayed, as rumored, the lack of an harmonious Venus-Mars tie may have contributed.

Even when Sun signs are compatible, if Sun/Moon ties are not, there may be problems in a marriage. This is dramatically shown in the charts of the Jazz Age lovers, authors F. Scott Fitzgerald and his wife Zelda. A fiery Leo like Jackie Kennedy, Zelda related well to her Air-sign husband, a romantic Libra. With his talent and her beauty and high spirits, they seemed to have everything on their side. Their Suns were compatible, so were their Moons. They even had a passionate Venus/Mars tie. Their Ascendants—the signs rising on the eastern horizon at their respective birthtimes—were in complementary opposite signs, often a sign of being meant for each other.

The problems that led to their separation probably stemmed from their Sun/Moon ties. His Sun was in disharmonious square to her Moon, and her Sun made the same type of aspect to his Moon. This set up a tension between them that was difficult to live with. She ended up in a mental hospital; he became an alcoholic. Together, they only reinforced the disharmony in their own charts.

Air Sign Romances

Air signs are intellectual, objective, and often not as romantic as Fire signs. Geminis can be fickle and changeable, Aquarians too freedom-loving to settle down, and Librans, while the most romantic of the Air signs, a bit cool at times. All three signs, however, share a sense of fun and curiosity that frequently bring them together in partnerships.

Air-sign natives Clark Gable and Carole Lombard were very close and will always be remembered as one of Hollywood's great romances. Her tragic death in a plane crash only a few years after their marriage added great poignancy to their romantic story.

Lombard was his perfect match in many ways, she a romantic Libra, he an Aquarius, their Suns in almost perfect trine. To add emotional depth to this union, both charts contained a strong water element. Lombard had a sensitive Pisces Ascendant and her Moon in Pisces; Gable had his Moon in emotional Cancer. They also had a good Mars/Venus tie that indicated physical passion.

More typical of many Air-sign romances, however, were the alliances entered into by England's merry monarch, King Charles II, who ruled that country during the slightly scandalous Restoration Period (1660–1685). With both Sun and Moon in variety-loving Gemini, this rakish king had mistresses by the dozen from all walks of life.

8

His two most famous mistresses, who captured his heart for longer periods of time than usual, were both born under Air signs. The first, Barbara Villiers, also known as "my lady Castlemaine," was a stately beauty, a Gemini like himself, with a romantic Libra Ascendant. Her Mars/Venus tie with him assured passion, but the intensity and possessiveness of her watery Scorpio Moon was ultimately too much for the lighthearted Gemini king.

Nell Gwyn, a witty Aquarian, also won his heart. Although she displayed many of the more boisterous, unconventional traits of Aquarius, her Sun in that sign was trine both his Sun and Moon. This little cockney girl, far below his station, won his heart and continued to fascinate him for seventeen years. He provided her with a fine home and servants, and requested on his death bed that she be looked after and not allowed to starve. Needless to say, there was a strong Mars/Venus tie between these two as well.

Earth Sign Romances

When Earth sign marries Earth sign, the accent is often on the practical or material side of life. These usually stable types generally have their feet on the ground and appreciate the reliability of another Taurus, Virgo, or Capricorn. They also relate well to the water signs, Cancer, Scorpio, and Pisces, providing a kind of stability for these more emotional types.

Love between Earth signs may be quiet and less dramatic or hectic than with the Air and Fire people, but these individuals tend to be very loyal and devoted over long periods of time, content to create comfortable homes together and attain security.

Of all the charts I've compared over the years, the ones who seemed most completely compatible belonged to two Earth-sign individuals — William Randolph Hearst and Marion Davies — who were never able to marry. They did create a home together, however, a splendid palace that remains a popular tourist attraction in California.

The charts of newspaper publisher William Randolph Hearst and his mistress, actress Marion Davies, provide an example of excellent compatibility in almost every way. He was a Taurus, with his Moon in Virgo; she a double Capricorn; both her Sun and Moon were trine his Sun and his Moon. Together they acquired many luxurious and unusual possessions which visitors can still view at the famous "Hearst Castle" in San Simeon.

While many in their era may not have approved of the unlegalized union of the newspaper magnate and the former chorus girl, their astrological compatibility was a perfect example of Ptolemy's rules about permanent alliances. Not only were all the Sun/Sun and Sun/Moon ties present, but Hearst's Venus conjunct her Mars, and her Venus trine his Mars added doubly passionate aspects to their relationship.

The money areas of their charts also complemented each other in remarkable ways. I'll have more to say about these two and their charts in Chapter Six, "Determining Mutual Money Luck."

A more sentimental and poetic union that the world remembers for its tenderness and depth of feelings occurred between Taurus Robert Browning and his water-sign love, poet Elizabeth Barrett Browning. Her love poems to him are famous. "How do I love thee, let me count the ways," begins the most well-known of the *Sonnets from the Portuguese*. What was the source of such transcendent love as she described?

The odds seemed all against this sickly, reclusive forty-year-old woman finding marriage, especially with a handsome, robust man six years her junior—a highly eligible bachelor. But something about the poetry she wrote compelled him to seek her out and become her friend, ultimately to carry her away from a dominating father to Italy where she regained her health.

What were the magnetic ties? First of all, his Taurus Sun was in harmonious sextile to her Pisces Sun; she would look upon him as good friend and a tower of strength. His Venus was trine her Mars; his Mars trine her Moon; he found her physically attractive even though she felt she was not. Her Venus was conjunct his Moon, adding to their mutual love, interests, and social harmony. Many other poetic ties between their charts, some of them that seemed karmic in nature, will be dealt with in later chapters. His love transformed her and brought her back to health.

Another Earth and Water duo, Fred Astaire and Ginger Rogers, were only screen lovers, but the magic they generated together on film stemmed in large part from the way their charts complemented each other. His earthy Taurus Sun was in harmonious sextile to her warmly feminine Cancer Sun, as well as to her sensitive Pisces Moon. His own Sun was not well-aspected by his own planets, but her Sun and Moon added strength and grace and drama to his Sun. Lately she has written that they did date in New York prior to their film careers. Unfortunately, there is an aspect between their charts, her Venus opposite his Uranus, that would create excitement, but also an urge to separate and be independent of each other.

Water Sign Lovers

When two Water signs get together, emotion rules the day. Elizabeth Taylor, one of the screen's most sensitive, romantic, Pisces women, whose Moon is in deeply emotional Scorpio, seemed to find the loves of her life in water-sign men. Mike Todd was a Cancer; Richard Burton a Scorpio. She is known to have had stormy arguments with both men, for there is often much temperament in the lives of water-sign people, especially if there are conflicting elements in their own charts.

Mike Todd had his Sun in warm, emotional Cancer trine to her sensitive Pisces Sun, but his Moon in dramatic Leo was square to her Scorpio Moon. They did not have close Venus/Mars aspects, although there were other elements of attraction, such as Venus conjunct Pluto. Even if he had not been killed in a plane crash, they ultimately might have been pulled apart by this Venus/Pluto conjunction in Cancer square to her Venus/Uranus conjunction in Aries.

With Burton, Taylor had many compatible Water-sign placements, but there were also oppositions to contend with. The Sun/Sun link in Water was there as well as the Sun/Moon tie of his Sun in Scorpio and her Moon in the same sign. His Moon in Virgo was opposite her Sun in Pisces, so he may have occasionally punctured her romantic moods with criticism. They had a close Venus/Mars tie, but also a Mars/Venus opposition. Their planets both brought them together and pulled them apart. No wonder they remarried after being divorced, then divorced again.

Julia Roberts and Lyle Lovett, both intense and passionate Scorpios, captured the hearts of many when they wed in a surprise ceremony in 1993. As this book goes to press, however, they have parted. They had an especially strong communication link with his Mercury conjunct hers in Scorpio. They had good Sun/Moon ties also. But her Venus and Mars are in Earth signs, while his Venus and Mars are in Fire and Air signs, not great for physical passion. It is his Neptune on her Sun that gave their romance a storybook quality.

Exceptions to the Sun/Sun Link

In my own studies of the charts of famous couples, I have observed that Ptolemy's formula holds true about Sun/Sun ties, but with a few exceptions. These exceptions are when the man and woman are members of adjoining Sun signs. The most usual side-by-side signs that seem to get along well are Gemini and Cancer, Virgo and Libra, and sometimes Aquarius and Pisces.

The chemistry between on-screen lovers Nelson Eddy and Jeanette MacDonald was an instance of one of these exceptions. Many who viewed them together in their series of musicals in the 1930s felt they were meant for each other. Actually, in many ways, they were. They were almost time-twins, having been born only eleven days apart. But she was a vivacious Gemini, he a devoted Cancer, members of side-by-side signs.

Some fans envisioned a real-life romance for them because of their great rapport in MGM film operettas. And there was much in their two horoscopes to indicate love and affection between them. Each had three planets in his Sun sign Cancer. Her Moon was there with his Sun, and in addition, there was a physically powerful Venus/Mars tie between the two.

With their birthdates only eleven days apart, the outer, slow-moving planets were in much the same positions in each chart. This magnified the difficult aspects each possessed as well as accented the affinities. Eddy's chart had a difficult and erratic Moon conjunct Uranus, and both opposed Pluto. Her Uranus opposite Pluto in the same positions only magnified the temperamental problems this may have caused. In addition, her Uranus/Pluto opposition was exactly squared by Mars, showing much temperament and strong will, earning her the label the "iron butterfly." Eddy's chart reinforced these qualities.

12

Was there really as much to their off-screen romantic feelings as their on-screen compatibility? They were teamed in eight film operettas between 1935 and 1942. During this time, each married, but to another person. In both cases, the marriage partner had a remarkable physical similarity of appearance to the other member of the screen duo. This led many of their fans to the conclusion that they really had been meant for each other. Their marriages were two years apart; their early deaths were also two years apart; the similarities in their horoscopes had much to do with this. Some people, however, felt he died of a broken heart after her premature death.

Another famous couple of that era who were members of the same side-by-side signs were the late Duke and Duchess of Windsor. Although he could have lived out his life as Edward VII of England, he renounced his throne to marry "the woman he loved," Wally Simpson, a divorcée from Baltimore. He was a devoted Cancer, she a light-hearted Gemini. Her Gemini joy-in-living seemed to bring him out of his shell and made her seem indispensible. By Sun sign they were quite different types; what was going for them astrologically?

First of all, he had four planets in Gemini. This helped a great deal. They had no Mars/Venus ties for great physical passion, but his Jupiter, the planet of generosity, made six wonderful aspects to her planets. This is the kind of set-up that will induce a person to do anything for another, deserved or not. In addition, Saturn, the planet of long-term responsibility and mature affection, also made six very good aspects to her planets. It may not have been the great love affair the world thought it to be, but an arrangement that provided comfort and stability for both.

In more recent times, the marriage of Connie Selleca, a Gemini, and John Tesh, a Cancer, repeats this Gemini/Cancer theme. She has Moon in Cancer to match his Water-sign Sun, while he has Moon in Aquarius to match her Air-sign Sun. In addition, they have her Mars and his Venus conjunct in Cancer, and his Venus and her Mars opposite each other from Taurus to Scorpio.

Another instance of side-by-side signs among the rich and famous is the long-term alliance of Paul Newman and Joanne Woodward. Although they are not of the same compatible element, they have karmic Sun/Moon ties that suggest soul mates. She is a sensitive member of the water element, Pisces. He is an airy Aquarius, but has his Moon in Pisces, exactly conjunct her Sun in Pisces by degree. She has her Moon in Aquarius, in the same sign as his Sun. Thus, they have the classic Sun/Moon ties that Ptolemy indicated would assure a lasting marriage.

In subsequent chapters, I'll show you how you can find these compatibility points between your horoscope and those of a lover. You'll also discover when your love planets will be "turned on" to bring the possibility of love or marriage into your life.

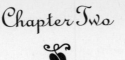

Chapter Two

When the Love Planets Are Most Likely to Attract Partners to Members of Your Sun Sign

Generally speaking, there are times when you should circulate more, knowing that the odds are in your favor when it comes to finding love and romance. We'll go more deeply into the subject of romantic timing on an individual level as the book progresses.

In this chapter, you'll find an overall picture of how the love planets will affect your Sun sign in the coming years. You'll discover the best times to visit more parties or groups, possibly working subtly into a conversation that old leading question, "What's your sign?" It's still the best way to determine basic compatibility.

Your Place in the Sun

You can always count on certain times of the year being most fortunate for you. This certainly applies to those periods when the transiting Sun makes a harmonious aspect to your natal Sun sign. A list of these times follows:

Fire and Air Signs

Aries: March 21 to April 19

Gemini: May 21 to June 21

Leo: July 22 to August 21

Libra: September 23 to October 22

Sagittarius: November 22 to December 21

Aquarius: January 21 to February 19

In general, if you were born during *one* of the above periods, you Fire and Air signs will find *any* of the above times especially harmonious for you.

Earth and Water Signs

Taurus: April 20 to May 20

Cancer: June 22 to July 21

Virgo: August 22 to September 22

Scorpio: October 23 to November 21

Capricorn: December 22 to January 20

Pisces: February 20 to March 20

Born in *one* of the above periods, you Earth and Water signs will find *any* of these especially harmonious times for you. Julia Roberts and Lyle Lovett, for example, found the Cancer period to be a happy romantic time. Both Scorpios, they married on June 27, 1993.

Venus and Mars as Romantic Timers

Unlike the Sun, the times that Venus and Mars occupy signs compatible to yours are different each year. But these are terrifically romantic times.

The most romantic time of all for you is during the yearly period when Venus, the planet of love, is transiting through your own sign. That's when you'll be at your charming best, attracting others to you, especially those who may become permanent romantic partners. In some cases, these may be persons you already know, whom you suddenly see in a new, more romantic light.

Also desirable are the times when Mars, the planet of passion, is traveling through your sign. Mars stays approximately two months in each sign, completing a cycle of the zodiac about every two years.

My research shows that the most promising time of all for finding a permanent love partner is when both Venus and Mars are traveling through your sign. Capricorns, for instance, could have been very lucky romantically in January, 1994, when Venus and Mars were exactly conjunct by degree in that sign.

This conjunction in Capricorn would also have been very favorable for the signs Virgo and Cancer, and almost as favorable for the other Earth and Water signs—Taurus, Scorpio, and Pisces.

If you'd like to research Venus and Mars in the same sign in your recent love life or in the romances of friends, relatives or celebrities—or see what's coming up romantically—at the end of this chapter, you'll find the times when Venus and Mars have been or will be in the same sign. Meanwhile, let's look at the Venus times of the year when you should be feeling very romantic and sociable.

Romantic Venus Times of the Year

The times when Venus is in your own sign vary a great deal each year, but they occur approximately one month out of twelve. When Venus is in your own sign, you'll glow with good looks and attract romance.

17

When Venus travels through the sign five signs from yours—
your solar fifth house of love and romance—you may be swept up
in a whirl of entertainment that can lead to love.

Then, when Venus is in the sign opposite yours in the zodiac—
your solar seventh house sign—you are likely to draw partnerships
to you. When Julia Roberts and Lyle Lovett took the world by
surprise with their sudden marriage, Venus was in Taurus, the
opposite sign for these two Scorpios. Venus was in the solar seventh house of marriage for both.

Another Scorpio who married when Venus was in Taurus was
Maria Shriver, who wed Arnold Schwarzenegger in April, 1986.
Venus, however, was in the fifth house of romance for Scorpio
actress Meg Ryan when she married actor Dennis Quaid on Valen-
tine's Day, 1991.

In looking at the Venus time periods that follow, look not only
for your own sign, but for the times when Venus is in the following
relation to your sign:

Your Sign	Your Romance Sign (Your 5th House)	Your Partner Sign (Your 7th House)
Aries	Leo	Libra
Taurus	Virgo	Scorpio
Gemini	Libra	Sagittarius
Cancer	Scorpio	Capricorn
Leo	Sagittarius	Aquarius
Virgo	Capricorn	Pisces
Libra	Aquarius	Aries
Scorpio	Pisces	Taurus
Sagittarius	Aries	Gemini
Capricorn	Taurus	Cancer
Aquarius	Gemini	Leo
Pisces	Cancer	Virgo

To a lesser extent, Venus is favorable for romance whenever it is in a sign that is compatible with yours: whenever Venus is in a Fire or Air sign if yours is a Fire or Air sign—or whenever Venus is in an Earth or Water sign if yours is an Earth or Water sign.

The lists that follow will show you the time periods when Venus is in the various zodiac signs during the coming years. These are shown in two separate lists, one for Fire and Air persons, the other for Earth and Water individuals. Remember when planning activities to give preference to your own sign first, then to your solar fifth and seventh house signs, for the most dynamic involvements.

Harmonious Venus Periods for Fire and Air Signs

1994

1/20 to 2/12	Aquarius
3/9 to 4/1	Aries
4/26 to 5/20	Gemini
6/15 to 7/10	Leo
8/8 to 9/7	Libra

1995

1/8 to 2/4	Sagittarius
3/3 to 3/27	Aquarius
4/22 to 5/16	Aries
6/11 to 7/4	Gemini
7/30 to 8/22	Leo
9/16 to 10/9	Libra
11/3 to 11/27	Sagittarius
12/22 to 12/31	Aquarius

1996

1/1 to 1/14	Aquarius
2/9 to 3/5	Aries
4/4 to 5/19	Gemini
5/20 to 7/1	Ge.—Venus retrograde
7/2 to 8/6	Gemini
9/7 to 10/3	Leo

1996 (cont.)

10/30 to 11/22	Libra
12/17 to 12/31	Sagittarius

1997

1/1 to 1/9	Sagittarius
2/3 to 2/26	Aquarius
3/23 to 4/15	Aries
5/11 to 6/3	Gemini
6/29 to 7/23	Leo
8/18 to 9/12	Libra
10/8 to 11/4	Sagittarius
12/12 to 12/25	Aquarius
12/26 to 12/31	Aq.—Venus retrograde

1998

1/1 to 1/9	Aq.—Venus retrograde
3/5 to 4/5	Aquarius
5/4 to 5/29	Aries
6/25 to 7/19	Gemini
8/13 to 9/6	Leo
10/1 to 10/24	Libra
11/18 to 12/11	Sagittarius

1999

1/5 to 1/28	Aquarius
2/22 to 3/17	Aries
4/13 to 5/8	Gemini
6/6 to 7/12	Leo
8/16 to 9/10	Leo — Venus retrograde
9/11 to 10/7	Leo
11/9 to 12/5	Libra
12/31	Sagittarius

2000

1/1 to 1/24	Sagittarius
2/18 to 3/12	Aquarius
4/7 to 4/30	Aries
5/21 to 6/18	Gemini
7/13 to 8/6	Leo
8/31 to 9/24	Libra
10/19 to 11/12	Sagittarius
12/8 to 12/31	Aquarius

2001

1/1 to 1/3	Aquarius
2/3 to 3/8	Aries
3/9 to 4/19	Ar. — Venus retrograde
4/20 to 6/6	Aries
7/6 to 8/1	Gemini
8/29 to 9/21	Leo
10/16 to 11/8	Libra
12/3 to 12/26	Sagittarius

2002

1/20 to 2/12	Aquarius
3/9 to 4/2	Aries
4/26 to 5/20	Gemini
6/15 to 7/10	Leo
8/7 to 9/8	Libra

2003

1/8 to 2/4	Sagittarius
3/3 to 3/27	Aquarius
4/22 to 5/16	Aries
6/11 to 7/4	Gemini
7/30 to 8/22	Leo
9/16 to 10/10	Libra
11/3 to 11/27	Sagittarius
12/23 to 12/31	Aquarius

2004

1/1 to 1/14	Aquarius
2/9 to 3/5	Aries
4/3 to 5/16	Gemini
5/17 to 6/28	Ge. — Venus retrograde
6/29 to 8/7	Gemini
9/7 to 10/3	Leo
10/30 to 11/22	Libra
12/17 to 12/31	Sagittarius

2005

1/1 to 1/9	Sagittarius
2/3 to 2/26	Aquarius
3/23 to 4/15	Aries
5/11 to 6/3	Gemini
6/29 to 7/23	Leo
8/18 to 9/11	Libra
10/9 to 11/5	Sagittarius
12/16 to 12/23	Aquarius
12/24 to 12/31	Aq. — Venus retrograde

2006

1/1 to 3/5	Aq. — Venus retrograde
3/6 to 4/6	Aquarius
5/4 to 5/29	Aries
6/25 to 7/19	Gemini

2006 (cont.)

8/13 to 9/6	Leo
10/1 to 10/24	Libra
11/18 to 12/11	Sagittarius

2007

1/6 to 1/28	Aquarius
2/22 to 3/17	Aries
4/13 to 5/8	Gemini
6/6 to 7/14	Leo
8/10 to 9/7	Leo — Venus retrograde
9/8 to 10/8	Leo
11/9 to 12/5	Libra
12/31	Sagittarius

2008

1/1 to 1/24	Sagittarius
2/18 to 3/12	Aquarius
4/7 to 4/30	Aries
5/25 to 6/18	Gemini
7/13 to 8/6	Leo
8/31 to 9/24	Libra
10/19 to 11/12	Sagittarius
12/8 to 12/31	Aquarius

2009

1/1 to 1/3	Aquarius
2/4 to 3/5	Aries
3/6 to 4/11	Ar. — Venus retrograde
4/25 to 6/6	Aries
7/7 to 8/1	Gemini
8/26 to 9/20	Leo
10/15 to 11/9	Libra
12/2 to 12/25	Sagittarius

2010

1/19 to 2/11	Aquarius

2010 (cont.)

3/8 to 3/31	Aries
4/26 to 5/20	Gemini
6/15 to 7/10	Leo
8/8 to 9/8	Libra
11/9 to 11/17	Lib. — Venus retrograde
11/18 to 11/30	Libra

2011

1/8 to 2/4	Sagittarius
3/3 to 3/27	Aquarius
4/22 to 5/15	Aries
6/10 to 7/4	Gemini
7/29 to 8/21	Leo
9/16 to 10/9	Libra
11/4 to 11/26	Sagittarius
12/21 to 12/31	Aquarius

2012

1/1 to 1/14	Aquarius
2/9 to 3/5	Aries
4/4 to 5/14	Gemini
5/15 to 6/26	Ge. — Venus retrograde
6/27 to 8/7	Gemini
9/7 to 10/3	Leo
10/29 to 11/22	Libra
12/17 to 12/31	Sagittarius

2013

1/1 to 1/9	Sagittarius
2/3 to 2/26	Aquarius
3/23 to 4/15	Aries
5/10 to 6/3	Gemini
6/28 to 7/22	Leo
8/17 to 9/11	Libra
10/8 to 11/5	Sagittarius

2014

3/6 to 4/5	Aquarius
5/4 to 5/29	Aries
6/24 to 7/18	Gemini
8/13 to 9/5	Leo
9/30 to 10/23	Libra
11/17 to 12/10	Sagittarius

2015

1/4 to 1/27	Aquarius
2/21 to 3/17	Aries
4/12 to 5/7	Gemini
6/6 to 7/18	Leo
8/1 to 9/5	Leo — Venus retrograde
9/6 to 10/8	Leo
11/9 to 12/5	Libra
12/31	Sagittarius

Harmonious Venus Periods for Earth and Water Signs

1994

1/1 to 1/19	Capricorn
2/13 to 3/8	Pisces
4/2 to 4/25	Taurus
5/21 to 6/14	Cancer
7/11 to 8/7	Virgo
9/8 to 10/18	Scorpio
10/19 to 11/22	Sco. — Venus retrograde
11/22 to 12/31	Scorpio

1995

1/1 to 1/7	Scorpio
2/5 to 3/2	Capricorn
3/28 to 4/21	Pisces
5/17 to 6/10	Taurus
7/5 to 7/29	Cancer
8/23 to 9/15	Virgo
10/10 to 11/2	Scorpio
11/28 to 12/21	Capricorn

1996

1/15 to 2/8	Pisces
3/6 to 4/3	Taurus

1996 (cont.)

8/7 to 9/6	Cancer
10/3 to 10/29	Virgo
11/23 to 12/16	Scorpio

1997

1/10 to 2/2	Capricorn
2/27 to 3/22	Pisces
4/16 to 5/10	Taurus
6/4 to 6/28	Cancer
7/24 to 8/17	Virgo
9/13 to 10/7	Scorpio
11/5 to 12/11	Capricorn

1998

1/10 to 2/4	Cap. — Venus retrograde
2/5 to 3/4	Capricorn
4/6 to 5/3	Pisces
5/29 to 6/24	Taurus
7/20 to 8/12	Cancer
9/7 to 9/30	Virgo
10/25 to 11/17	Scorpio
12/12 to 12/31	Capricorn

1999

1/1 to 1/4	Capricorn
1/29 to 2/21	Pisces
3/18 to 4/12	Taurus
5/9 to 6/5	Cancer
7/13 to 7/29	Virgo
7/30 to 8/15	Vir. — Venus retrograde
10/8 to 11/8	Virgo
12/6 to 12/30	Scorpio

2000

1/25 to 2/17	Capricorn
3/13 to 4/6	Pisces
5/1 to 5/20	Taurus
6/19 to 7/12	Cancer
8/7 to 8/30	Virgo
9/25 to 10/18	Scorpio
11/13 to 12/7	Capricorn

2001

1/4 to 2/2	Pisces
6/7 to 7/5	Taurus
8/2 to 8/28	Cancer
9/22 to 10/15	Virgo
11/9 to 12/2	Scorpio
12/7 to 12/31	Capricorn

2002

1/1 to 1/19	Capricorn
2/13 to 3/8	Pisces
4/2 to 4/25	Taurus
5/21 to 6/14	Cancer
7/11 to 8/6	Virgo
9/9 to 10/9	Scorpio
10/10 to 11/20	Sco. — Venus retrograde
11/21 to 12/31	Scorpio

2003

1/1 to 1/7	Scorpio
2/5 to 3/2	Capricorn
3/28 to 4/21	Pisces
5/17 to 6/10	Taurus
7/5 to 7/29	Cancer
8/23 to 9/15	Virgo
10/11 to 11/2	Scorpio
11/28 to 12/22	Capricorn

2004

1/15 to 2/8	Pisces
3/6 to 4/2	Taurus
8/8 to 9/6	Cancer
10/4 to 10/29	Virgo
11/23 to 12/16	Scorpio

2005

1/10 to 2/2	Capricorn
2/27 to 3/22	Pisces
4/16 to 5/10	Taurus
6/4 to 6/28	Cancer
7/24 to 8/17	Virgo
9/12 to 10/8	Scorpio
11/6 to 12/15	Capricorn

2006

1/2 to 2/2	Cap. — Venus retrograde
2/3 to 3/5	Capricorn
4/7 to 5/3	Pisces
5/30 to 6/24	Taurus
7/20 to 8/12	Cancer
9/7 to 9/30	Virgo
10/25 to 11/17	Scorpio
12/12 to 12/31	Capricorn

23

2007

1/1 to 1/5	Capricorn
1/29 to 2/21	Pisces
3/18 to 4/12	Taurus
5/9 to 6/5	Cancer
7/15 to 7/25	Virgo
7/26 to 8/9	Vir. — Venus retrograde
10/9 to 11/8	Virgo
12/6 to 12/30	Scorpio

2008

1/25 to 2/17	Capricorn
3/13 to 4/6	Pisces
5/1 to 5/24	Taurus
6/19 to 7/12	Cancer
8/7 to 8/30	Virgo
9/25 to 10/18	Scorpio
11/13 to 12/7	Capricorn

2009

1/4 to 2/3	Pisces
4/12 to 4/16	Pis. — Venus retrograde
4/17 to 4/24	Pisces
6/7 to 7/6	Taurus
8/2 to 8/25	Cancer
9/21 to 10/14	Virgo
11/10 to 12/1	Scorpio
12/26 to 12/31	Capricorn

2010

1/1 to 1/18	Capricorn
2/12 to 3/7	Pisces
4/1 to 4/25	Taurus
5/21 to 6/14	Cancer
7/11 to 8/7	Virgo
9/9 to 10/7	Scorpio

24

2010 (cont.)

10/8 to 11/8	Sco. — Venus retrograde
12/1 to 12/31	Scorpio

2011

1/1 to 1/7	Scorpio
2/5 to 3/2	Capricorn
3/28 to 4/21	Pisces
5/16 to 6/9	Taurus
7/5 to 7/28	Cancer
8/22 to 9/15	Virgo
10/10 to 11/3	Scorpio
11/27 to 12/20	Capricorn

2012

1/15 to 2/8	Pisces
3/6 to 4/3	Taurus
8/8 to 9/6	Cancer
10/4 to 10/28	Virgo
11/23 to 12/16	Scorpio

2013

1/10 to 2/2	Capricorn
2/27 to 3/22	Pisces
4/16 to 5/9	Taurus
6/4 to 6/27	Cancer
7/23 to 8/16	Virgo
9/12 to 10/7	Scorpio
11/6 to 12/20	Capricorn
12/21 to 12/31	Cap. — Venus retrograde

2014

1/1 to 1/30	Cap. — Venus retrograde
1/31 to 3/5	Capricorn
4/6 to 5/3	Pisces
5/30 to 6/23	Taurus
7/19 to 8/12	Cancer

2014(cont.)

9/6 to 9/29	Virgo
10/24 to 11/16	Scorpio
12/11 to 12/31	Capricorn

2015

1/1 to 1/3	Capricorn
1/28 to 2/20	Pisces

2015(cont.)

3/18 to 4/11	Taurus
5/8 to 6/5	Cancer
7/19 to 7/24	Virgo
7/25 to 7/31	Vir. — Venus retrograde
10/9 to 11/8	Virgo
12/6 to 12/30	Scorpio

The periods marked Venus retrograde are special times when Venus appears to move in reverse direction from our viewpoint on earth. These are not good times for initiating new romantic contacts or giving parties. They are best for working on a love relationship to improve it. Often someone from your past will show up at this time to either renew a relationship or attempt to. At such times, relationships may break up, or temporary new ones begin. There may be revisions in your views about love and marriage.

Passionate Mars Times of the Year

When Mars is in your sign, approximately every two years, your energies and passions are heightened, and romantic involvement is more likely. When Mars is in a sign compatible to yours, love relationships are also more probable.

As mentioned above, when both Mars and Venus are in your sign, you are most likely to find a relationship that ends in marriage. This is also true when both Venus and Mars are in signs compatible to your sign.

A good principle to follow is this: When one of the love planets—Venus or Mars—is in a sign compatible to yours, but the other is in an incompatible sign, you are more likely to meet—or suddenly fall for—someone who is incompatible to you by Sun sign. This is because one of you will be under the influence of Venus and the other under the influence of Mars.

I have seen numerous examples of this principle. For example, when Edward T., a Cancer, met Ellen L., an Aries, Venus was in

25

Scorpio, compatible to Edward's sign, while Mars was in Leo, compatible to Ellen's Aries sun. They married, but with Sun signs square to each other, the marriage didn't last.

A similar incompatible romance resulted when an Aquarian man met a Virgo woman when Venus was in Gemini. Aquarius and Virgo often seem to relate in mental ways, but are not compatible by sign. With Venus in the man's solar fifth house, highly compatible to his Sun sign, he was in the mood for a fling, possibly even more than one with Gemini involved. Mars, the planet of passion, was in Cancer, the home-loving sign favorable to the woman's Virgo Sun. The attraction was strong, but it didn't have a chance of lasting.

If you're looking for a long-term, happy love, look for those dates when both Venus and Mars are in compatible signs for you. Then you are more likely to meet someone who is compatible by sign.

Find your best Mars periods in the list below, using the same procedures you did for Venus. Then look for the times when both Mars and Venus are harmonious to your Sun sign.

Harmonious Mars Periods for Fire and Air Signs

1994
1/28 to 3/6	Aquarius
4/15 to 5/23	Aries
7/4 to 8/16	Gemini
10/5 to 12/11	Leo

1995
1/23 to 3/23	Leo — Mars retrograde
3/24 to 5/25	Leo
7/21 to 9/6	Libra
10/21 to 11/30	Sagittarius

1996
1/8 to 2/14	Aquarius
3/25 to 5/2	Aries
6/13 to 7/25	Gemini
9/10 to 10/29	Leo

1997
1/3 to 2/5	Libra
2/6 to 3/8	Lib. — Mars retrograde
6/19 to 8/13	Libra
9/29 to 11/8	Sagittarius
12/18 to 12/31	Aquarius

1998
1/1 to 1/24	Aquarius
3/5 to 4/12	Aries
5/24 to 7/5	Gemini
8/21 to 10/7	Leo
11/27 to 12/31	Libra

1999
1/1 to 1/26	Libra
5/6 to 6/3	Lib. — Mars retrograde

1999 (cont.)

6/4 to 7/4	Libra
9/3 to 10/16	Sagittarius
11/26 to 12/31	Aquarius

2000

1/1 to 1/4	Aquarius
2/12 to 3/22	Aries
5/4 to 6/16	Gemini
8/1 to 9/16	Leo
11/4 to 12/23	Libra

2001

2/15 to 5/10	Sagittarius
5/11 to 7/18	Sag. — Mars retrograde
7/19 to 9/8	Sagittarius
10/28 to 12/8	Aquarius

2002

1/19 to 3/1	Aries
4/14 to 5/28	Gemini
7/14 to 8/29	Leo
10/17 to 12/1	Libra

2003

1/18 to 3/4	Sagittarius
4/23 to 6/18	Aquarius
12/17 to 12/31	Aries

2004

1/1 to 2/3	Aries
3/22 to 5/7	Gemini
6/24 to 8/10	Leo
9/28 to 11/11	Libra
12/26 to 12/31	Sagittarius

2005

1/1 to 2/6	Sagittarius
3/22 to 5/1	Aquarius

2005 (cont.)

6/13 to 7/28	Aries

2006

2/18 to 4/14	Gemini
6/4 to 7/22	Leo
9/9 to 10/23	Libra
12/6 to 12/31	Sagittarius

2007

1/1 to 1/16	Sagittarius
2/27 to 4/6	Aquarius
5/16 to 6/24	Aries
8/8 to 9/28	Gemini

2008

1/1 to 1/29	Gem. — Mars retrograde
1/30 to 3/4	Gemini
5/10 to 7/1	Leo
8/20 to 10/4	Libra
11/17 to 12/27	Sagittarius

2009

2/5 to 3/15	Aquarius
4/23 to 5/31	Aries
7/13 to 8/25	Gemini
10/17 to 12/19	Leo
12/20 to 12/31	Leo — Mars retrograde

2010

1/1 to 3/9	Leo — Mars retrograde
3/10 to 6/7	Leo
7/30 to 9/14	Libra
10/29 to 12/7	Sagittarius

2011

1/16 to 2/23	Aquarius
4/3 to 6/4	Aries
6/22 to 8/3	Gemini

27

2011 (cont.)
9/20 to 11/11 Leo

2012
7/4 to 8/23 Libra
10/8 to 11/17 Sagittarius
12/27 to 12/31 Aquarius

2013
1/1 to 2/2 Aquarius
3/13 to 4/20 Aries
6/1 to 7/13 Gemini
8/29 to 10/15 Leo
12/8 to 12/31 Libra

28

2014
1/1 to 3/1 Libra
3/2 to 5/19 Lib. — Mars retrograde
5/20 to 7/26 Libra
9/14 to 10/26 Sagittarius
12/5 to 12/31 Aquarius

2015
1/1 to 1/12 Aquarius
2/21 to 3/31 Aries
5/13 to 6/24 Gemini
8/9 to 9/25 Leo
11/13 to 12/31 Libra

Harmonious Mars Periods for Earth and Water Signs

1994
1/1 to 1/27 Capricorn
3/7 to 4/14 Pisces
5/24 to 7/3 Taurus
8/17 to 10/4 Cancer
12/12 to 12/31 Virgo

1995
1/1 to 1/2 Virgo
1/3 to 1/22 Vir. — Mars retrograde
5/26 to 7/20 Virgo
9/7 to 10/20 Scorpio
12/1 to 12/31 Capricorn

1996
1/1 to 1/7 Capricorn
2/15 to 3/24 Pisces
5/3 to 6/12 Taurus
7/26 to 9/9 Cancer
10/30 to 12/31 Virgo

1997
1/1 to 1/2 Virgo
3/9 to 4/27 Vir. — Mars retrograde
4/28 to 6/18 Virgo
8/14 to 9/28 Scorpio
11/9 to 12/17 Capricorn

1998
1/25 to 3/4 Pisces
4/13 to 5/23 Taurus
7/6 to 8/20 Cancer
10/8 to 11/26 Virgo

1999
1/27 to 3/17 Scorpio
3/18 to 5/5 Sco. — Mars retrograde
7/5 to 9/2 Scorpio
10/17 to 11/25 Capricorn

2000
1/5 to 2/11 Pisces

2000 (cont.)

3/23 to 5/3	Taurus
6/17 to 7/31	Cancer
9/17 to 11/3	Virgo
12/24 to 12/31	Scorpio

2001

1/1 to 2/14	Scorpio
9/9 to 10/27	Capricorn
12/9 to 12/31	Pisces

2002

1/1 to 1/18	Pisces
3/2 to 4/13	Taurus
5/29 to 7/13	Cancer
8/30 to 10/16	Virgo
12/2 to 12/31	Scorpio

2003

1/1 to 1/17	Scorpio
3/5 to 4/22	Capricorn
6/19 to 7/28	Pisces
7/29 to 9/26	Pis. — Mars retrograde
9/27 to 12/16	Pisces

2004

2/4 to 3/21	Taurus
5/8 to 6/23	Cancer
8/11 to 9/27	Virgo
11/12 to 12/25	Scorpio

2005

2/7 to 3/21	Capricorn
5/2 to 6/12	Pisces
7/29 to 10/1	Taurus
10/2 to 12/9	Tau. — Mars retrograde
12/10 to 12/31	Taurus

2006

1/1 to 2/17	Taurus
4/15 to 6/3	Cancer
7/23 to 9/8	Virgo
10/24 to 12/5	Scorpio

2007

1/17 to 2/26	Capricorn
4/7 to 5/15	Pisces
6/25 to 8/9	Taurus
9/29 to 11/14	Cancer
11/15 to 12/31	Can. — Mars retrograde

2008

3/5 to 5/9	Cancer
7/2 to 8/19	Virgo
10/5 to 11/16	Scorpio
12/28 to 12/31	Capricorn

2009

1/1 to 2/4	Capricorn
3/16 to 4/22	Pisces
6/1 to 7/12	Taurus
8/26 to 10/16	Cancer

2010

6/8 to 7/29	Virgo
9/15 to 10/28	Scorpio
12/8 to 12/31	Capricorn

2011

1/1 to 1/15	Capricorn
2/24 to 4/2	Pisces
6/5 to 6/21	Taurus
8/4 to 9/19	Cancer
11/12 to 12/31	Virgo

2012

1/1 to 1/23	Virgo

2012 (cont.)

1/24 to 4/13	Vir. — Mars retrograde
4/14 to 7/3	Virgo
8/24 to 10/7	Scorpio
11/18 to 12/26	Capricorn

2013

2/3 to 3/12	Pisces
4/21 to 5/31	Taurus
7/14 to 8/28	Cancer

2013 (cont.)

10/16 to 12/7	Virgo

2014

7/27 to 9/13	Scorpio
10/27 to 12/4	Capricorn
1/13 to 2/20	Pisces
4/1 to 5/12	Taurus
6/25 to 8/8	Cancer
9/26 to 11/12	Virgo

The Mars retrograde periods, similar to Venus retrograde periods, are not as favorable for making new contacts, but may bring back old lovers into your life, or may call for new attitudes and actions on your part.

Periods When Venus and Mars Occupy the Same Sign in Coming Years

As mentioned above, these are the most potent periods of all for the signs they affect. Look back to see how they have affected your love life, or forward, to see how they might in the future. If the conjunction is in your own sign, all the better. If both Mars and Venus are in a Fire or Air sign, you Fire and Air signs benefit. If in an Earth or Water sign, you Earth and Water signs are most likely to find romance.

1990

1/30–3/3	Capricorn	Earth
3/12–4/5	Aquarius	Air
4/21–5/3	Pisces	Water

1991

5/9–5/26	Cancer	Water
6/6–7/10	Leo	Fire
7/16–8/21	Virgo	Earth

1992

1/1–1/8	Sagittarius	Fire
1/31–2/17	Capricorn	Earth
2/19–3/13	Aquarius	Air
3/28–4/6	Pisces	Water

1993

12/3–12/19	Sagittarius	Fire

1994
12/27 (93)–1/19 Capricorn Earth
1/28–2/12 Aquarius Air
3/7–3/8 Pisces Water

1995
10/10–10/20 Scorpio Water
11/3–11/27 Sagittarius Fire
12/1–12/21 Capricorn Earth

1996
1/8–1/14 Aquarius Air
6/13–7/25 Gemini Air
8/7–9/6 Cancer Water
9/10–10/3 Leo Fire

1997
9/12–9/28 Scorpio Water
10/8–11/4 Sagittarius Fire
11/9–12/11 Capricorn Earth

1998
12/18 (97)–1/9 Aquarius Air
6/25–7/5 Gemini Air
7/20–8/12 Cancer Water
8/21–9/6 Leo Fire

2000
5/1–5/3 Taurus Earth
5/26–6/16 Gemini Air
6/19-7/12 Cancer Water
8/1–8/6 Leo Fire

2002
4/2–4/13 Taurus Earth
4/26–5/20 Gemini Air
5/29–6/14 Cancer Water
12/2–1/7 (03) Scorpio Water

2003
1/18–2/4 Sagittarius Fire

2004
3/6–3/21 Taurus Earth
4/4–5/7 Gemini Air
10/30–11/11 Libra Air
11/23–12/16 Scorpio Water

2005
12/26–1/9 (06) Sagittarius Fire

2006
9/7–9/8 Virgo Earth
10/1–10/23 Libra Air
10/25–11/17 Scorpio Water
12/7–12/11 Sagittarius Fire

2009
8/7–8/19 Virgo Earth
8/31–9/24 Libra Air
10/5–10/18 Scorpio Water
4/9–4/22 Pisces Water
4/25–5/31 Aries Fire
6/7–7/5 Taurus Earth
7/13–8/1 Gemini Air
8/26 (1 day only) Cancer Water

2010
7/11–7/29 Virgo Earth
8/8–9/8 Libra Air
9/15–10/28 Scorpio Water

2011
4/22–5/11 Aries Fire
5/16–6/9 Taurus Earth
6/22–7/5 Gemini Air

31

2013

2/27–3/12	Pisces	Water
3/23–4/15	Aries	Fire
4/21–5/9	Taurus	Earth
6/1–6/3	Gemini	Air

2015

1/4–1/12	Aquarius	Air
1/28–2/20	Pisces	Water
2/21–3/17	Aries	Fire
4/1–4/11	Taurus	Earth
8/9–9/25	Leo	Fire
10/9–11/8	Virgo	Earth
11/13–12/5	Libra	Air

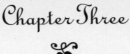

Chapter Three

What You Need in a Marriage Partner

What are the traits you'd like in a marriage partner? One person might say, "A sense of humor, good dancer, financially successful, an extrovert." Another might prefer "A quiet, sensitive type who writes sentimental love notes, who is loyal and stable." A third might find important "a good figure, sexy glance, or someone who shares an interest in travel."

Individual preferences are important. And, possibly more than you imagine, these preferences appear in your birth chart, easy for a trained astrologer to spot. If you don't think so, try this out. Before you go any further in this chapter, set down on paper a list of what you really want in a mate. Then later match it with the preferences you'll find your chart indicates.

Personality, appearance, emotional, mental, and romantic attitudes on your list will probably match what your chart shows you want—or will attract. If there are conflicts in your mind, these conflicts will appear in your chart also. Just glance at the squares and oppositions between your marriage-indicator planets and signs to see the conflicts.

There may, however, be some hidden desires about a potential mate that you have repressed, desires which you or society might not approve. If a man, it may be hard to admit you're looking for a substitute mother. But if you have the Moon (a mother symbol) in your seventh house of partners, that's what you often end up with. A woman may not realize she's looking for a father figure, but if Saturn is associated with her seventh house, she may unconsciously seek older men or authority figures for mates.

Even worse, a woman may not realize that she's looking for a man of violence or an alcoholic. But if Mars or Neptune afflict her seventh house, she may unconsciously bring such conditions into her life. That is, until she becomes more aware of her role in what she's attracting.

Once aware, she can consciously look for men who represent the higher sides of the planets involved. With Neptune, for instance, instead of those addicted to drugs or alcohol, she can seek a mate who's an artist, musician, actor, or highly spiritual.

What Your Chart Has to Say About a Mate

The Rising Sign (Ascendant) or first house of your chart describes you. The seventh house (the pie-shaped area of the wheel directly across from the first) describes the kind of partners you tend to attract. Any planets in the seventh house help describe your mates.

In addition, the planet that rules the sign on your seventh house cusp also describes that mate, not only by traits, but by its sign and house position in your chart. This house ruler becomes especially important when there are no planets in your seventh house.

The four love planets described in Chapter One — Sun, Moon, Venus, and Mars — also indicate preferences in love and marriage.

In a man's chart, it has been traditional to find his feminine ideal through looking at the sign, house, and aspects of his Moon and Venus. In a woman's chart, we find her masculine ideal through examining her Sun and Mars.

How to Blend Contradictory Planets and Signs

You'll frequently find contradictions in the story told by one's seventh house plus the love planets representing the opposite sex. For instance, Mars in Capricorn in a woman's chart might indicate that she likes steady, reliable practical men. But if her Sun is in Aries, she may also be dazzled by charming, dynamic heartbreakers, always looking for new conquests. Then, she may have the buttoned-down sign Virgo on the seventh house cusp, with its ruler, Mercury, in daredevil Aries. Just what kind of man *is* she likely to attract?

She may be more than a little in conflict over just what qualities she actually wants. At times, she may attract Aries men, at other times, Capricorns or Virgos. She'll be most likely to settle down with a man whose chart contains some of the same contradictions that are in her own. He might be a Capricorn, with Aries rising and Moon in Virgo.

Or the signs themselves may not be so much represented as the qualities they portray. Capricorn could represent a businessman, traditionalist, or father figure. Aries might suggest, in addition, that this man be a brave, ambitious type, who can be rather reckless or daring at times in his business dealings. The Virgo qualities might make him a hard worker, one who gains great satisfaction from his job.

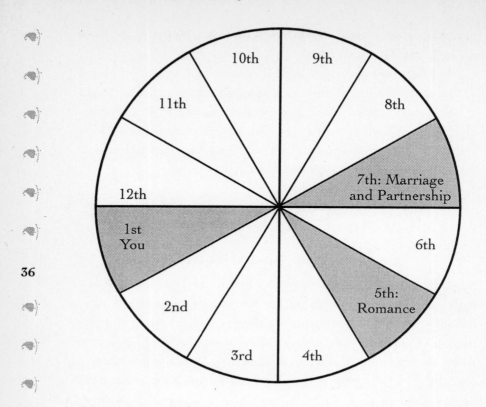

The Twelve Houses of the Astrological Chart

Where to Find Marriage and Romance in a Chart

There are twelve houses—symbolizing various areas of one's life—in every astrological chart. The sectors of marriage and romance are listed below and illustrated above.

The first house: You

The fifth house: Romance

The seventh house: Marriage and Partnership

The Contradictions in Elizabeth Taylor's Chart

Someone who has married a great many times, like Elizabeth Taylor, provides a fine example of such contradictory messages.

With romantic Libra rising, the sign on her seventh house cusp is Aries. Sometimes she would like daring, dynamic Aries-type men. Mike Todd was one of these, not an Aries by Sun sign, but a tough-talking entrepreneur who pioneered dazzling endeavors. In Taylor's chart, contradictions begin to show up when we look at the ruler of her seventh house. It is Mars in Pisces. Here it suggests a gentle, sensitive man, a real romantic at heart. Todd also must have had this side to him, since he was born under the gentle Water sign of Cancer.

Taylor had the planets Venus and Uranus in her seventh house. This impulsive, love-at-first-sight combination in the marriage house has contributed to her many marriages. Among her eight husbands were men as impulsive as she in plunging into controversial relationships. Richard Burton was typical. Their affair, which began during the filming of *Cleopatra* while she was still married to Eddie Fisher, is a good example.

In addition, Taylor's Sun, the other indicator of men in her life, is in Pisces along with Mars. Pisces suggests not only sensitivity, but singers, entertainers, and, on the negative side, escapists and alcoholics. Since Sun and Mars are in the fifth house, the natural house of Leo, which rules show business, it's no wonder that she attracted such men as Eddie Fisher and Richard Burton. Both were in the entertainment world, Eddie Fisher was a Leo, and both at times in their lives had problems with drink or drugs. Burton was, in addition, a Scorpio, a Water sign like Pisces.

Her latest husband, Larry Fortensky, had a similar problem. They met at the Betty Ford Center for the treatment of such addictions. He was a construction worker, which fulfills the rough, tough Aries seventh house cusp, but he is undoubtedly sensitive also and caring, fulfilling her need for men who reflect the Water element.

Finding the Partner in Your Zodiac

To help you assemble the traits that make up your ideal mate, fill out the form below as you study your horoscope. If you do not have a natal chart, it's easy to send for one from one of the computer services (see Appendix A, page 151).

As you list the signs and planets that apply to your chart, remember that all of these indications may not be equally valid at any one time. You may never have even dated a member of the Sun sign on your seventh house cusp, but that sign can indicate qualities you look for in each potential mate you meet.

Let's begin to assemble the portrait of Mr. or Ms. Right. For an interpretation of what each of these signs and planets mean in the context of a partner, see the list of traits at the end of this chapter. First, fill out the form. Then look up the meanings in the section which follows. When you blend all the characteristics, you'll find they probably correspond rather closely to the list you made at the start of this chapter.

Ideal Mate Form

1. What is the sign on your seventh house cusp? _____.

2. List any planets in the seventh house:_____.

3. What is the planetary ruler of the sign on your seventh house cusp? _____ (see a list of rulers below).

4. In what sign and house is this ruler? _____ in _____.

5. If male, what is your Moon sign and house? _____ in _____. What is your Venus sign and house? _____ in _____.

6. If female, what is your Sun sign and house? _____ in _____. What is your Mars sign and house? _____ in _____.

The Rulers of each Sign

If you need help finding the rulers of each sign, they are listed below.

Aries is ruled by Mars	Libra is ruled by Venus
Taurus is ruled by Venus	Scorpio is ruled by Pluto
Gemini is ruled by Mercury	Sagittarius is ruled by Jupiter
Cancer is ruled by the Moon	Capricorn is ruled by Saturn
Leo is ruled by the Sun	Aquarius is ruled by Uranus
Virgo is ruled by Mercury	Pisces is ruled by Neptune

Romantic Traits in Your Chart

Aries / Mars — If the sign Aries or the planet Mars are partner indicators in your chart (or if one of your mate-indicator planets is in the first house), you could attract someone who is aggressive, outgoing, socially sparkling, passionate, impulsive, quick, competitive, ardent, or dynamic. If this planet or sign is negatively aspected in your chart (by a square or opposition), this person might be self-centered, demanding, and lacking in refinement. This person may have been born under one of the Fire signs—Aries, Leo, or Sagittarius—have Aries rising or Mars in their first house, or be very muscular, active, involved in sports, or engaged in an other than sedentary occupation.

Taurus / Venus — If the sign Taurus or the planet Venus are partner indicators in your chart (or if one of your mate-indicator planets is in the second house), you could be drawn to someone who is emotionally loyal, steadfast, persistent, stable, sensual, money-minded, artistic, a lover of beauty and luxury, with a heightened sense of touch. If this planet or sign is negatively aspected in your chart (by a square or opposition), traits such as selfishness, laziness, or stubbornness may manifest. This person would tend to attract rather than pursue love, and can have been born under one of the Earth signs—Taurus, Virgo, or Capricorn. They may have

Taurus rising, or Venus in their first house, or be rather passive and comfort-loving and engaged in a sedentary occupation.

Gemini / Mercury — If the sign Gemini or the planet Mercury are partner indicators in your chart (or if one of your mate-indicator planets is in the third house), you could be fascinated by someone who is friendly, witty, talkative, variety-loving, versatile, intellectual, a good writer, dancer, or speaker, quick on their feet, and who tends to fall in love with your mind first. If this planet or sign is negatively aspected in your chart (by a square or opposition), traits such as inconsistency, fickleness, and unreliability may manifest. This person would tend to approach you in a friendly manner, flirt, or come to you for information, and can have been born under one of the Air signs—Gemini, Libra, or Aquarius. They may have Gemini rising, or Mercury in their first house, or be someone who makes a living through communication or transportation.

Cancer / Moon — If the sign Cancer or the Moon are partner indicators in your chart (or if one of your mate-indicator planets is in the fourth house), you could attract someone who is nurturing, romantic, deeply sensitive, moody, home-loving, protective, domestic, receptive, impressionable, and sympathetic. If this planet or sign is negatively aspected in your chart (by a square or opposition), this person might be easily hurt, maudlin, and their feelings might fluctuate like the Moon. This person may have been born under one of the Water signs—Cancer, Scorpio, or Pisces—have Cancer rising or Moon in their first house, or be very much interested in food, cooking, and feeding others, and be generally sensitive to public needs. They may be engaged in an occupation that serves others in some nurturing way.

Leo / Sun — If the sign Leo or the Sun are partner indicators in your chart (or if one of your mate-indicator planets is in the fifth house), you could attract someone who is ardent with fixed affections, creative, romantic, dramatic, theatrical, generous, magnetic, fun-loving, dignified, and born to rule or manage. If this planet or sign is negatively aspected in your chart (by a square or opposition), this person might be dominating, egotistical, and require not only center stage, but constant praise and applause. This person may have been born under one of the Fire signs—Leo, Sagittarius, or Aries—have Leo rising or Sun in their first house, or be very dramatic and proud, love to speculate and gamble, or be engaged in a management or theatrical occupation.

Virgo / Mercury — If the sign Virgo or the planet Mercury are partner indicators in your chart (or if one of your mate-indicator planets is in the sixth house), you could attract someone who is efficient, mental, modest, discriminating, analytical, practical, helpful, and hard-working. If this planet or sign is negatively aspected in your chart (by a square or opposition), this person might be critical, lacking in warmth, too selective, a hypochondriac, or a workaholic. This person might be a co-worker or interested in sharing tasks with you, might be especially health-conscious, neat, and clean. The occupation could involve papers, writing, service to others, the medical field, or some manual skill.

Libra / Venus — If the sign Libra or the planet Venus are partner indicators in your chart (or if one of your mate-indicator planets is in the seventh house), you may attract someone who is attractive, marriage-minded, eager to please, romantic, sociable, refined, smiling, affectionate, and aesthetic with a love of music, art, and beauty. If this planet or sign is negatively aspected in your chart (by a square or opposition), this person might be superficial, indecisive, either too argumentative or too quick to give in, or lazy and content with not making waves. This person would tend to attract rather than pursue love, but would be eager to pair up in a partnership rather than do things alone. They could have been born under Libra, or one of the other Air signs—Gemini and Aquarius—or may have Libra rising or Venus in the first house. They may be engaged in an occupation in which keeping things in balance, diplomacy, socializing, or artistic values are involved.

Scorpio / Pluto — If the sign Scorpio or the planet Pluto are partner indicators in your chart (or if one of your mate-indicator planets is in the eighth house), you could be drawn to someone who is deeply emotional, passionate, sexy, mysterious, powerful, idealistic, intense, strong, and resourceful. If this planet or sign is negatively aspected in your chart (by a square or opposition), you might find yourself with someone who is manipulative, too secretive, obsessive, resentful, jealous, and who may go to extremes. This person may have been born under Scorpio or one of the other Water signs — Cancer and Pisces — have Scorpio rising or Pluto in the first house. They may be interested in occult or esoteric subjects, in large corporations, or in researching into unknown territories. Their occupation may involve transforming others in some way, medical science, or reforming existing ills.

Sagittarius / Jupiter — If the sign Sagittarius or the planet Jupiter are partner indicators in your chart (or if one of your mate-indicator planets is in the ninth house), you may attract someone who is optimistic, friendly, vivacious, gregarious, frank and open, interested in sports, travel, religion, higher education, and the great outdoors. If this planet or sign is negatively aspected in your chart (by a square of opposition), this person might be blunt, outspoken, dogmatic about beliefs, excessive in some way, and idealistically impractical. This person might have been born under Sagittarius or one of the other fire signs — Aries and Leo — or have Sagittarius rising or Jupiter in the first house. The occupation may involve travel, publishing, law, religion, or teaching.

Capricorn / Saturn — If the sign Capricorn or the planet Saturn are partner indicators in your chart (or if one of your mate-indicator planets is in the tenth house), you could be drawn to someone who is older, an authority figure, ambitious, hard-working, disciplined, stable, responsible, and more sexy than expected. If this planet or sign is negatively aspected in your chart (by square or opposition), traits such as pessimism, lack of generosity, snobbishness, or opportunism may surface. This might result in a marriage of convenience or for money and status. Although your partner is often older when you are young, this is frequently reversed when you are older, and you may become the Saturnian partner. Your mate may be a Capricorn or born under one of the other Earth Signs—Taurus and Virgo. Or they may have Capricorn rising or Saturn in their first house. They may be engaged in an occupation that is routine, orderly, and can involve much ambition.

Aquarius / Uranus — If the sign Aquarius or the planet Uranus are partner indicators in your chart (or if one of your mate indicator planets is in the eleventh house), you may attract someone who is independent, original, futuristic and intellectual, unconventional, a friend to all, and possibly a genius. If this planet or sign is negatively aspected in your chart (by a square or opposition), traits such as unreliability, eccentricity, or rebelliousness may manifest, or there could be sudden partings. Your mate would tend to be an Aquarius—or one of the other Air Signs—Gemini or Libra—or have Aquarius rising or Uranus in their first house. The occupation might involve technology, computers, broadcasting, or astrology.

Pisces / Neptune — If the sign Pisces or the planet Neptune are partner indicators in your chart (or if one of your mate indicator planets is in the twelfth house), you could bring someone into your life who is sensitive, compassionate, secretive, intuitive, imaginative, dreamy, musical, artistic, psychic, and can be extremely romantic and sentimental. If this planet or sign is negatively aspected in your chart (by a square or opposition), this person may be hypersensitive, unrealistic, deceptive, fearful, a recluse or martyr, or involved in some sort of unhealthy escape from life such as drink or drugs. This person would tend to attract rather than pursue love, and might be a Pisces or be born under one of the other Water signs—Cancer, and Scorpio. They might have Pisces rising or Neptune in their first house, or be engaged in an occupation such as singing, dancing, acting, art, photography, films, or other sensitive, imaginative pursuits.

Your Fifth House of Romance

Sometimes one attracts romantic partners based on the fifth house of romance that do not reflect anything about your seventh house of marriage. Generally, marriage does not result when only the fifth house indicators are involved. So if the indications for this house by planet and sign are quite different from your seventh house, you may find yourself marrying someone who is a good mate (seventh house), but not necessarily a romantic partner (fifth house). It's wise to look also at the indications shown by the planets in your fifth house and by the ruler of this house. Then attempt to blend some of these indications with the seventh house choices.

Further Messages Your Love Planets Contain

This section is for those who would like to discover the more detailed information about a potential mate that is found in the degrees of each sign. Each sign of the zodiac is divided into three sections—or decanates—each containing ten degrees. Each of these decanates is ruled by a planet and sign. Each sign of the zodiac is also divided into twelve duads, based on the twelve signs of the zodiac. See the following tables for a list of the decanates and duads of each sign.

If you are a woman, you might look at the degree of your Sun or Mars, for instance, and see what further information about a potential mate you can find from the decanates and duads of each sign. For example, a woman with her Sun at 25 degrees of Virgo has her Sun in the Taurus decanate and the Cancer duad. Her first husband was a Taurus; her second, a Virgo with Moon in Cancer.

Decanates

Sign	0–10°	10–20°	20–30°
Aries	Aries	Leo	Sagittarius
Taurus	Taurus	Virgo	Capricorn
Gemini	Gemini	Libra	Aquarius
Cancer	Cancer	Scorpio	Pisces
Leo	Leo	Sagittarius	Aries
Virgo	Virgo	Capricorn	Taurus
Libra	Libra	Aquarius	Gemini
Scorpio	Scorpio	Pisces	Cancer
Sagittarius	Sagittarius	Aries	Leo
Capricorn	Capricorn	Taurus	Virgo
Aquarius	Aquarius	Gemini	Libra
Pisces	Pisces	Cancer	Scorpio

Duads

Degrees / Signs	0 to 2.5	2.5 to 5	5 to 7.5	7.5 to 10	10 to 12.5	12.5 to 15	15 to 17.5	17.5 to 20	20 to 22.5	22.5 to 25	25 to 27.5	27.5 to 30
Aries (Ar)	Ar	Ta	Ge	Cn	Le	Vi	Li	Sc	Sa	Cp	Aq	Pi
Taurus (Ta)	Ta	Ge	Cn	Le	Vi	Li	Sc	Sa	Cp	Aq	Pi	Ar
Gemini (Ge)	Ge	Cn	Le	Vi	Li	Sc	Sa	Cp	Aq	Pi	Ar	Ta
Cancer (Cn)	Cn	Le	Vi	Li	Sc	Sa	Cp	Aq	Pi	Ar	Ta	Ge
Leo (Le)	Le	Vi	Li	Sc	Sa	Cp	Aq	Pi	Ar	Ta	Ge	Cn
Virgo (Vi)	Vi	Li	Sc	Sa	Cp	Aq	Pi	Ar	Ta	Ge	Cn	Le
Libra (Li)	Li	Sc	Sa	Cp	Aq	Pi	Ar	Ta	Ge	Cn	Le	Vi
Scorpio (Sc)	Sc	Sa	Cp	Aq	Pi	Ar	Ta	Ge	Cn	Le	Vi	Li
Sagittarius (Sa)	Sa	Cp	Aq	Pi	Ar	Ta	Ge	Cn	Le	Vi	Li	Sc
Capricorn (Cp)	Cp	Aq	Pi	Ar	Ta	Ge	Cn	Le	Vi	Li	Sc	Sa
Aquarius (Aq)	Aq	Pi	Ar	Ta	Ge	Cn	Le	Vi	Li	Sc	Sa	Cp
Pisces (Pi)	Pi	Ar	Ta	Ge	Cn	Le	Vi	Li	Sc	Sa	Cp	Aq

When the Planets Overhead Make Lucky Aspects to Your Natal Love Planets: The Transits

To find out when love could come to you, you'll need to have a copy of your horoscope and an ephemeris to check where the outer planets are going to be in the next few years.

The movements of the planets around the skies have a direct relationship to the romantic opportunities that appear in your life. You've already learned something about that in Chapter Two. Now we go a step farther and apply this information not just to your Sun sign, but to the placements of the other planets at your birth.

As you learned in Chapter Two, when Venus is in your own sign, you glow with special charm that attracts romance and sociability. When Venus contacts one of your love planets, there's even more of an upsurge in your romantic and social life.

The transits most likely to produce dramatic love events or changes in your life are, however, those from the outer planets — Jupiter, Saturn, Uranus, Neptune, and Pluto.

When one of these planets overhead is at a point in the zodiac where it forms a favorable conjunction, trine, or sextile to one of your love planets, get ready for romance.

The planet in transit that contacts one of these degrees determines the nature of the romantic event. Pluto usually brings passion and deep radical changes; Neptune, beautiful events, ideals, or spiritual love; Uranus, surprise, change, and excitement; Saturn, stability and loyalty; Jupiter, generosity and adventure. Each of the planets in transit brings a different message, and the love planet it contacts, another.

48

How to Find Your Love Planets

Look for the planets that occupy your natal fifth house of romance or your natal seventh house of marriage — or that rule these houses, plus romantic Venus and passionate Mars. In Chapter Three you used your love planets to determine the type of partner you would attract. Now you can use these same planets to find romantic opportunities.

I like to use Elizabeth Taylor's chart to illustrate love planets because she had so many of them. Half of her ten planets were love planets. In her fifth house of romance she had Mars, Sun, and Mercury in Pisces. In her seventh house of marriage Venus was conjunct Uranus in Aries. With Aries the sign on her seventh cusp, Mars ruled this house. This planet, at 2 degrees of romantic Pisces, is in her fifth house of love affairs.

Mars thus has triple importance as a love planet. It is in the fifth house, rules the seventh house and is one of the general love planets. Whenever one of the outer planets transited to a zodiac degree in conjunction, sextile, or trine Mars, it stimulated a romantic situation in her life.

The sensitive points in her chart to Mars were conjunctions at 2 degrees of Pisces, trines at 2 degrees of Scorpio and 2 degrees of Cancer, and sextiles at 2 degrees of Capricorn and 2 degrees of Taurus. In her case, an outer planet transiting through one of these degrees practically guaranteed marriage bells.

Any competent astrologer who looked at her chart when she was a baby would have found it simple to predict when her first celebrated marriage would take place. An ephemeris for the years following her birth on February 27, 1932, shows the first outer planet to reach a trine to her Mars is Uranus. By 1950, when she was 18, it had traveled from 18 degrees of Aries in her seventh house to 2 degrees of Cancer in her ninth house of legalization. In addition, that same year, Jupiter had reached 2 degrees of Pisces, where it conjoined natal love planet Mars.

Just as the planets indicated, Liz was wed on May 6, 1950. Her first husband was hotel heir Nicky Hilton. Theirs was a Uranian/Jupiterian type of marriage; it was a grand, showy affair that captured many headlines, but didn't last long.

Impulsive Uranus is very important in her love life. It rules her fifth house and is located in the seventh, like Mars, tying together love and marriage in her horoscope. Conjunct the planet of love, Venus, we have an indication here of one who often falls in love at first sight and marries quickly and easily.

Whenever a planet in transit contacted the conjunction of Venus and Uranus in Liz' seventh house of marriage, sudden changes occurred in her love life. This romantic combination, at 17 and 18 degrees of fiery Aries, would be trined by any planet reaching 17–18 degrees of Sagittarius or 17–18 degrees of Leo.

Natally, Liz had the planet of good luck, Jupiter, at 15 degrees of Leo, very near one of these sensitive spots. When she married for the first time, the planet Pluto had traveled from her tenth house to her eleventh and was conjunct Jupiter.

49

This meant that three outer planets—Pluto, Uranus, and Jupiter—were in aspect to her love planets at the time of her first marriage. There was great romantic pressure to marry *someone* at age 18. (Although these were the main transits indicating a wedding, there are always also progressions and converse directions that act as timers when a marriage year arrives. We'll cover these other timers in the next chapter.)

In Taylor's subsequent marriages, the outer planets went on to transit other significant degrees of the zodiac in relation to her natal love planets. When Neptune arrived at 2 degrees of Scorpio in 1957, Liz married Mike Todd. Uranus had drawn near to that degree in 1975 when Liz took a second stab at marital bliss with Richard Burton.

Although there were variations in the patterns of the aspects, an outer planet had only to draw near to one of her romantic zodiacal degrees for romantic news about Liz to grab the headlines.

How to Plot Your Own Romance Patterns

Discovering your own best romantic times of your life is not too difficult. They will most likely coincide with the favorable conjunction, trine, and sextile transits of the slow-moving outer planets, Pluto, Neptune, Uranus, Saturn, or Jupiter to your love planets.

If it looks like forever until one of these transits will get to the right place in your chart, don't overlook opportunities when faster-moving Sun, Moon, Mercury, Venus, or Mars are making trines or sextiles to your love planets. Since these planets often set off progressions at your romance degrees, you may be pleasantly surprised. (More about progressions in the next chapter.)

Don't forget that any Venus transit can become a love transit, even if it isn't aspecting a planet connected with your fifth or seventh house. Venus, remember, is the planet of love.

When to Take Care in Your Love Life

There are also negative degrees in the zodiac in relation to your love planets. These are the points from which a transiting planet squares or opposes one of your love planets. Be aware of these and ready for challenges. When an outer planet passes over one of these points, it can sometimes indicate a break-up or rearrangement of an existing relationship or a short-lived romance complete with conflicts that could rival any soap opera.

Sometimes, however, you get a double message, when a negative love transit occurs at the same time as a positive one. This usually shows that there can be obstacles to overcome. Liz Taylor had such an aspect on March 15, 1964, when she married Richard Burton the first time. Uranus in transit was opposing both her Sun and Mercury in the fifth house.

Uranus is often a planet of break-ups. Here, it probably indicated that both Taylor and Burton had to defy conventions and break up their existing marriages in order to wed.

Directions for Finding Your Romantic Times

If you haven't already listed your love planets, here's a good way to keep track of them and the harmonious times when they'll be activated. First, take a copy of your birth chart and circle with red each of these:

1. Any planets in your natal fifth or seventh houses.
2. The planets that rule your fifth or seventh houses.
3. Venus and Mars, wherever they may be.

Next, write down the degrees and sign of your love planets. These degrees, as you have seen from the above examples, will be very

51

responsive to any transit in bringing Mr. or Ms. Right into your life. List also the degree and sign of your Ascendant and Descendant. These are also very sensitive points where relationships are concerned.

Then, list the degrees which are trine and sextile to the above places in the zodiac. If you need help in finding trines and sextiles, you can use the tables below. For a love planet at 10 degrees of Taurus, for instance, trines to it would be at or around 10 degrees of Virgo and Capricorn. Sextiles to it would be at 10 degrees of Pisces and Cancer.

Signs	Trines	Sextiles
Aries	Leo, Sagittarius	Aquarius, Gemini
Taurus	Virgo, Capricorn	Pisces, Cancer
Gemini	Libra, Aquarius	Aries, Leo
Cancer	Scorpio, Pisces	Taurus, Virgo
Leo	Sagittarius, Aries	Gemini, Libra
Virgo	Taurus, Capricorn	Cancer, Scorpio
Libra	Gemini, Aquarius	Leo, Sagittarius
Scorpio	Cancer, Pisces	Virgo, Capricorn
Sagittarius	Aries, Leo	Libra, Aquarius
Capricorn	Taurus, Virgo	Scorpio, Pisces
Aquarius	Gemini, Libra	Sagittarius, Aries
Pisces	Cancer, Scorpio	Capricorn, Taurus

If you list the harmonious places in zodiacal order, starting at zero degrees Aries and ending with 29 degrees of Pisces, you can handle the project more effectively. Then you can look through the outer planets' places in the Appendix or an ephemeris, glancing at a month at a time. Write down all dates when a planet in transit is at one of these points.

It would be wise to also list on a separate sheet of paper any squares or oppositions to your love planets. Then you can be ready for any challenges in your love life.

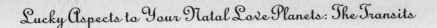

Previewing Your Love Life in the Months Ahead

The transiting planets that are contacting your own love planets can tell you a great deal about the types of persons, situations, and emotions which will be in your romantic life. This applies also to the planets which may be passing through your fifth or seventh houses.

A Pluto transit, for instance, might bring someone with a strong Scorpio nature, possibly an individual with a Scorpio Sun, Moon, Ascendant, or with Pluto in the first house. Pluto might also bring jealousy or power plays. A Uranus transit might bring a sudden, unexpected love affair. Jupiter could bring someone with money, or a traveler, while Venus might manifest a sociable, warm-hearted individual. Here's a more complete run-down on what you can expect.

Powerful Pluto's Romantic Effects

Pluto — When slow-moving, powerful Pluto aspects one of your romance planets, there may be radical changes in your love life. These will usually help you grow in some way. There are various manifestations possible. You could experience a renewal of passions with a current lover or an intense Scorpionic type of new lover. With harmonious contacts from Pluto, any changes in your love life will be easier, almost magical. If Pluto squares or opposes a romantic planet (and often when it conjuncts), a more traumatic situation may ensue. There could be a break with the past in some way, power struggles, jealousies, and attempts of one lover to dominate the other. These can lead to real growth when you become willing to let go of that part of the past which is no longer valid in your life.

These same conditions may apply during the years when Pluto travels through your fifth house of romance or your seventh house of partners. During these periods, you may run into Scorpio types,

53

individuals who are secretive but deeply emotional, or partners who change your life in some dramatic way. Pluto works slowly, but the effects of its transits can suddenly break to the surface with great drama and intensity.

Nebulous Neptune in your Love Life

Neptune — Neptune in aspect to your love planets casts a magical spell over affairs of the heart. You become more responsive to poetry, beauty, music, or escapist activities. You may dream a great deal, read about romance, or watch sentimental films. In harmonious aspect to one of your love planets, Neptune is likely to inspire, elevate, or create beautiful hopes and illusions. Even in good aspect, Neptune may find you projecting an idealized view of reality upon everything around you, including the one you adore. In challenging aspect, however, Neptune really zaps you with unrealistic expectations. Be careful you don't set yourself up for heartaches or disappointments by pursuing an unrealizable dream. Check out reality every now and then or you may be fooled or led astray. Secret romances and intrigue are also possible. Sometimes the "secret love" you feel is difficult to reveal even to the one you care about.

The kinds of persons you're apt to be drawn to when Neptune transits through your fifth or seventh houses include Pisces types, musicians, artists, spiritual leaders, and sensitive individuals of all kinds. Be watchful, however, to steer clear of any deceptive, escapist, or alcoholic persons who may appear during these periods.

The Excitement of Uranus

Uranus — Uranus in good aspect to one of your love planets brings a much different message. You can look forward to excitement, change, and greater independence in your love life. Be prepared also for breathtaking sudden flings, love at first sight, or unexpected turns of affairs that cause you to break loose of some former inhibitions. Not only will you feel more independent and daring, but you'll attract these same qualities in those you encounter. If, however, transiting Uranus is in square or opposition to one of your love planets, watch out for hit-and-run affairs or even break-ups of a current relationship. While a good relationship can survive such bids for change and independence, do be prepared for something unexpected to happen. It's a good time to add variety to old routines that may have grown dull.

The periods when Uranus travels through your fifth house of romance or your seventh house of partners, are likely to be romantically quite unusual. You may attract someone of a different age who seems like an equal. You'll see more of Aquarians, unusual or unconventional types, and those who like their independence. Quite often, you may encounter those who bring, or accompany, changes in your life. A lover may be involved in astrology, computers, or science. This person is likely to want to bring new ways of thinking to your life and could show up in your life through a group to which you belong. Expect the unexpected with this love, including surprise calls, dates, and behavior.

Saturn and Stability

Saturn — With Saturn, however, you can expect greater stability. When this planet transits your love planets through trine or sextile, you tend to be more realistic, responsible, and clear-headed about your love life. Long-term partnerships are entered into more willingly, and someone who is practical, mature, and down-to-earth will look good to you. More challenging, however, are the times when Saturn conjuncts, squares, or opposes romance planets. A lesson you need to learn about partnerships will be presented to you, testing your ability to be responsible, to discipline yourself, or to overcome obstacles. Or you may attract individuals who prove to be burdens in some way.

When Saturn travels through your fifth house of romance or your seventh house of partners, you may go through a period when you attract Saturnian types—those who are much older (or younger), more mature, or more serious-minded. One of you is apt to act more like a parent than equal to the other.

Jupiter and Good Fortune in Love

Jupiter — Jupiter is the Santa Claus of the zodiac, bestowing ease and good fortune when in harmonious aspect to one of your love planets. Relationships are often accompanied by wealth, travel, expansion, or a feeling of optimism and generosity. Any obstacles seem easy to overcome. Even when in a challenging square or opposition, Jupiter can bring good luck. The only danger is that you may be over-optimistic or self-indulgent, throwing caution to the winds. Since Jupiter rules belief systems, this can also be an indication that you and a mate will not agree on your basic philosophies of life.

56

During the periods when Jupiter transits through your fifth or seventh houses, you're likely to meet Sagittarians, or happy-go-lucky, carefree types. You'll attract generosity, persons who live and think in a prosperous manner, or travelers, foreigners, lawyers, and persons who teach, publish, advertise, think big, and are likely to philosophize about life.

Lesser Indications of a Big Romance

Transits from the inner planets that follow are less likely to indicate, all by themselves, a giant conflagration in your love life, but they may be setting off a progression or accompanying an outer planet transit, so I'll include the meanings here.

Mars and Passion

Mars — The transit of Mars to your love planets sends passions and desires soaring. You'll face romance as an exciting challenge, exhibiting energy, action, and aggressiveness in your love relationships. Or, you may attract a bold, courageous individual who plays this role. At its best, Mars will stir you into action to meet or to wed the object of your affection.

When in square or opposition, however, Mars can stir up conflict, arguments, or a lack of sensitivity to the feelings of others. Often, passion is mixed with a desire to win someone's heart for the sake of winning. Since transiting Mars circles your chart once every two years, it moves too fast to be significant all by itself. As mentioned above, it is mainly important when triggering a slower transit or a solar arc or progression.

You'll find that when Mars travels through your fifth or seventh houses, you will encounter impulsive Aries types or persons of great energy, daring, and physical strength. Although usually passionate, the Mars types are often blunt and given to argue or compete with you at the drop of a hat.

Venus, the Love Planet Supreme

Venus — As you discovered in Chapter Two, you'll feel more beautiful, handsome, and romantic when Venus occupies important places in your horoscope. When in your first house or Sun sign, for instance, you'll glow with those warm-hearted, special qualities that attract love. When Venus is in harmonious conjunction, trine, or sextile to your romance planets, you'll radiate romantic feelings. The world will seem a more beautiful place, people will be kinder, and your response to these good feelings is more likely than usual to attract admirers.

Since Venus aspects these planets about once a year, its transit is more important as a good time for entertaining, dating, or expressing sentimental feelings than for world-shaking romantic events. (By the much slower-moving progressions, however, it's one of the prime indications of marriage times.) In disharmonious aspect, Venus transits cause little trouble. A bit of self-indulgence, laziness, or social awkwardness is the worst one can expect.

The people you will attract into your life when Venus transits your fifth or seventh houses will tend to be beautiful, loving, artistic, and kind, possessing many of the qualities of the two Venus-ruled signs, Taurus and Libra.

Mercury and Mental Appeal

Mercury — You'll talk and think more about romance when Mercury aspects one of your love planets. Phone calls and invitations via the mail could be more plentiful. You'll be more likely to travel here and there and meet interesting prospects who have a great deal to say.

Naturally, communication with loved ones will be more important when Mercury travels through fifth or seventh houses. Gemini and Virgo types, those who are clever, witty, and amusing to have around should show up. Sharing meaningful ideas could be more important even than physical passion. You might fall in love head- first, rather than heart-first.

The Ever-Changing Moon

Moon — The Moon moves so quickly around the zodiac that its effects are momentary. Slower-moving planets, however, can be triggered by the passage of the Moon in aspect to one of your romance planets. The mood may be more romantic when the Moon moves through the fifth or seventh houses, but for any really meaningful event, aspects from progressions or slower-moving transits will be needed.

The Illuminating Sun

Sun — As you discovered in Chapter Two, transits of the Sun are important in indicating generally harmonious periods for you. They also act as timers, setting off slower-moving transits and progressions. A Sun transit is more likely to indicate a significant day if it is working in conjunction with other aspects to one of your love planets.

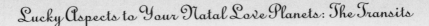
New Moons and Eclipses

New Moons / Eclipses — When the transiting Sun and Moon conjoin in a New Moon or a solar eclipse, the resultant aspects and houses affected become much more significant. Therefore, a New Moon or eclipse in your fifth or seventh houses should give one notice that much action is to be expected in the romantic and partnership areas of life.

With a New Moon in one of these houses, you will be making a new start in a love relationship in the coming month. An eclipse in one of these houses indicates a period of at least several months when major activity could be centered around love and marriage and the people who play important roles in your life.

59

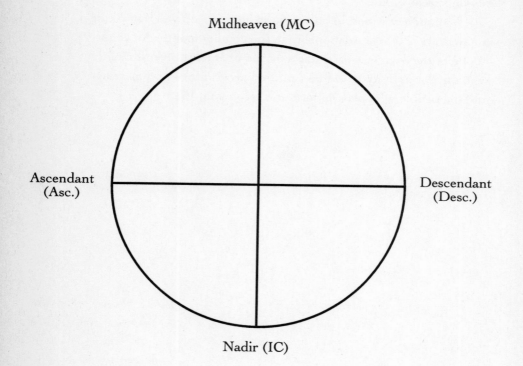

Power Points — The Four Angles in a Chart

Chapter Five

A Compatibility Check-up With Someone You've Met

Each planet in your chart symbolizes some phase of you or your life. Venus, for instance, represents love, beauty, art, and socializing. If you run into someone at a party who shares no Venus links with you, don't expect natural affection to develop. You'll probably sit and talk about the weather or excuse yourself to find the powder room.

If you find some area in common, it will depend on other aspects between your two sets of planets. Both your Moons might be in Cancer, for example, and you might feel linked by Moonchild subjects like family, recipes, or children. But without Venus aspects between your charts—or with challenging aspects to your Venus from that other person's planets, don't expect to develop a bosom buddy friendship.

For an enduring relationship such as marriage, it's very necessary that certain links between planets be present, especially the "big four" love links—Sun, Moon, Venus, and Mars. We discussed those in Chapter One. In this chapter, I'm going to show you an easy way to compare each planet in your chart with each planet in a potential mate's chart.

First of all, however, you need to know just what each planet symbolizes in terms of a relationship. These planets have additional meanings in other areas of life. But to read a chart for love links, it's best to focus on the following meanings.

The Planets in Relationships

Sun — This represents how you like to express your individuality in a relationship. This is the part of you that needs strokes for the ego and recognition of the self as a unique person. A mate who has good aspects to your Sun will recognize your importance more than someone who does not. The sign your Sun is in will make a great difference as to the traits which you will wish to be appreciated for. An Aries might wish appreciation for being first, for winning, for daring, dash, and fire. A Virgo, however, might be more pleased to know that a mate goes for his or her efficiency, literary interests, or mastery of details. That's why it's important that you marry a compatible sign. The Sun also expresses the masculine side of life. If you are a woman, it rules the men in your life. If you are a man, it has to do with your own feelings of masculinity. A man who becomes involved with a woman who has only challenging aspects to his Sun—or no aspects at all—can receive little reinforcement of or appreciation of his masculine side from such a partner. Thus a man *must have* good aspects to his Sun from the woman in his life.

Moon — Your emotions, feelings, home life, family, domestic inclinations, imagination, sensitivity, karmic past, subconscious mind, women in your life, and type of responses in general are ruled by the Moon. You'll feel "at home" with a partner whose Moon is in sync with yours. If you are a woman, you'll respond with intuition and understanding to a man whose masculine Sun makes good aspects to your feminine Moon. Someone who says, "My mate doesn't understand me," (if it isn't just a line) may be married to someone whose planets make no good aspects to his or her Moon. If someone's restrictive Saturn is in conjunction, square, or opposition to your Moon, you may feel unable to express your real emotions around this person. If you are a woman, you especially need a man whose planetary aspects to your Moon make you feel more feminine.

Mercury — Since this planet rules your mind, style of communication, ideas, and self-expression, harmonious aspects to your Mercury from a mate's chart will lead to the feeling you can really share ideas and relate well conversationally. Without good aspects, or with no real aspects, to your Mercury, you may be at a loss for the right words or may feel you have nothing to talk about together. With really challenging aspects to your Mercury from a mate's planets, you may find your ideas misunderstood, leading to pointless quarrels and differences of opinion. Since communication is often one of the prime keys to a good relationship, make sure your Mercurys are in sync, especially to the other's Mercury, Sun, Moon, or Jupiter.

Venus — The sign Venus is in shows what you love, how you like to socialize, your romantic style, aesthetic interests, and governs feelings of spontaneous affection between persons. In a man's chart, it indicates the type of women he goes for. If his Venus is in Aries, he might appreciate a sports-loving, competitive career woman. But if his Venus is in Cancer, he'd be more apt to desire a domestic, mothering, home-loving type. You want to make sure that you share good Venus aspects with a mate, whether you are male or female. Venus to Mars aspects show physical attraction. Venus to Sun and Venus to Venus are also very good. Adverse Venus aspects may play havoc with your love life.

63

Mars — Mars is the planet of action and aggressiveness. In a relationship, the sign your Mars is in indicates your style of action, passion, and the amount or kind of combativeness in your nature. A pair who have good Mars to Mars links possess similar energy patterns and styles of behavior; they go into action of any kind with harmony. Mars in good aspect with other planets in a partner's chart will add to attraction and will help you accomplish projects smoothly as a team. Some of the most challenging relationship patterns are set up, however, when many Mars aspects square or oppose your planets from another's chart. This can lead to quarrels and constant dissension. In a woman's chart, as we have learned in Chapter Three, Mars equates with the type of man she likes, as does the Sun.

64

Jupiter — Since Jupiter represents luck, benevolence, generosity, and rewards, you should be so fortunate as to have a nice Jupiter aspect to any of your planets from a partner's Jupiter. That person who is always on your side, no matter what, probably has a Jupiter conjunction, sextile, or trine to one of your planets. The area of life that will receive benefits can be seen by the planet, sign, and house that their Jupiter aspects. A Jupiter square or opposition is not quite so favorable, but may increase a tendency to overdo in some area of the relationship. It may also indicate a partner who is willing to over-indulge or spoil you. But since Jupiter rules one's belief systems and philosophy of life, there may be profound basic differences in these areas if two Jupiters are inharmonious to each other. While adverse Jupiter aspects seldom cause serious rifts in a relationship, they can be minor irritants at times.

Saturn — Responsibilities, burdens, security urges, age differences, and karmic ties are often shown by Saturn aspects between charts. "Restrictive Saturn" is quite the opposite of "generous Jupiter" in nature. But good aspects from another's Saturn, such as trines and sextiles, may help you to gain self-discipline and grow. Such a person is often able to see where you need greater self-discipline and will be able to let you know in a way that really helps. A negative Saturn aspect, which includes the conjunction as well as the square and opposition, does not have to be bad, but may cause another to be critical of you at times in a way that makes you resist their advice. It might also cause you delays, add to low self-esteem, or restrict you in some way. A Saturn conjunction to one's Sun or Moon may sometimes seem to represent a karmic tie that includes some problem to be worked out together.

Uranus — In a relationship, Uranus can represent attraction, excitement, fascination, and falling in love at first sight. But this planet in aspect to one of your planets may also bring sudden changes and instability. The conjunction to one of your love planets — Sun, Moon, Venus, or Mars — can be very stimulating, but may represent a transitory affair. Trines or sextiles from Uranus to your planets are more long-range in nature, and can create almost as much fascination. Squares and oppositions should alert you to be on your guard because they could represent nothing more than a fling.

Neptune — This planet of beauty and illusion can symbolize the very highest, most idealistic kinds of love ties. But don't count on it. Sometimes Neptune makes things look too good to be true. Since Neptune is the planet of ESP and magic, ties from another's Neptune to your planets or vice versa may feel karmic and fated. You may be instinctively able to read each other's minds and understand what is unspoken. Watch out for the squares and oppositions, however, from a mate's Neptune to your planets. These are the most likely to cause confusion, illusion, or even outright deception — although often it is self-deception.

Pluto — In a relationship, Pluto deepens ties, adds passion and sexual intensity, but also may represent power plays, violence, and jealousy or possessiveness. Pluto aspects to your personal planets are especially indicative of strong emotions and sexual drives. Watch out for the squares and oppositions, however. These are where the more harmful side of Pluto may emerge from the depths of a relationship. Examine carefully any adverse aspects between one person's Mars and another's Pluto. These are usually the most predictive of difficult relationships.

The Angles in Relationship

The four angles are power points in any chart. They are the Ascendant, Descendant, Midheaven, and Nadir; they contain the greatest power when a planet—either natal, progressed, or in transit—is conjunct (see illustration on page 60).

Ascendant — The degree and sign on the Eastern horizon at the time you were born represents your Ascendant. Anything or anyone born at that moment of time will possess the characteristics of that sign and degree, at least as far as the outward appearance and method of greeting or approaching the world. It equates with dawn, beginnings, new starts, and in your chart, you and your personality, your method of presenting yourself. Those who have good aspects to the degree and sign of your Ascendant relate well to you personally. They may appreciate you, your looks, and personality especially well.

Midheaven — The highest point overhead at the moment you were born is called the Midheaven. The sign and degree culminating on the Midheaven at the moment of birth symbolizes one's public standing, career, and reputation. It equates with noontime when the Sun is most commanding and magnificent. If you desire a mate who will back you in career moves or enhance your public standing, find someone whose planets make beneficial conjunctions, trines, or sextiles to your Midheaven.

Descendant — The point opposite your Ascendant is the Descendant. It represents partnerships in your life. Someone whose Sun, Moon, Venus, or Jupiter conjoins or is in good aspect to this point will seem like a natural partner to you.

Nadir or IC — The lowest point in a chart, the Nadir or IC, symbolizes your home, family, and most basic self. You'll see in Chapter Five how aspects to the IC can signify karmic ties from the past, since this is the point that represents where you enter and leave your current life. Favorable aspects to this point in your chart are excellent if you want to share a home together. You may seem meant for each other in some way, as if you've always known each other, but don't remember where or when.

Chart Comparison Step-by-Step

Although you may have the charts of you and a partner before you, it's not always easy to see all the aspects between them right away, without a little practice. It helps if you list the planets and their degrees side by side. If you have access to a computer program that lists the aspects between two charts for you, use it to get the basic trines, squares, etc., but then copy the planets in order on the form shown on page 69 so that you can get an organized overview of where each planet is in relation to the partner's planets.

To show how this works, let's list the planetary aspects between the charts of two famous lovers, Richard Burton and Elizabeth Taylor. Obviously, this was not a perfect union, because they ultimately separated, but it must have held a great deal of fascination because they married each other twice. Their list of planets and angles side-by-side follows.

Planets	Burton's Planets Degree & Sign	Taylor's Planets Degree & Sign
Sun	17° Scorpio	8° Pisces
Moon	11° Virgo	26° Scorpio
Mercury	7° Sagittarius	8° Pisces
Venus	4° Capricorn	18° Aries
Mars	28° Libra	2° Pisces
Jupiter	18° Capricorn	15° Leo
Saturn	17° Scorpio	0° Aquarius
Uranus	21° Pisces	17° Aries
Neptune	24° Leo	6° Virgo
Pluto	14° Cancer	20° Cancer

Angles

Asc.	16° Cancer	3° Libra
Desc.	16° Capricorn	3° Aries
MC	13° Pisces	4° Cancer
IC	13° Virgo	4° Capricorn

How To Find The Aspects

Although a computer program that compares charts will give you the aspects between two charts, you can also find them easily with the following information.

Conjunctions

Conjunctions are the easiest aspects to find. They are within 10 degrees of each other in the same sign. In the lists above, you'll note that Burton's Venus is at 4 degrees of Capricorn and Taylor's IC is at 4 degrees of Capricorn. This is an exact conjunction, making it especially strong. Since Venus is the planet of love and the IC rules the past, this may have indicated a karmic love from the past.

Conjunctions Not in the Same Sign

Sometimes conjunctions are not in the same sign, however. Remember there are only 30 degrees in each sign. Burton's Mars is at 28 degrees of Libra. Any planet within 10 degrees of this would still be conjunct, even if in the next sign. In this case a planet in from 18 degrees of Libra to 8 degrees of Scorpio (the next sign) would be conjunct to his Mars at 28 degrees of Libra. Similarly, a planet in early degrees of a sign, such as Taylor's Mars at 2 degrees of Pisces, can be considered conjunct with a planet in from 22 degrees of Aquarius, the preceding sign, up to 12 degrees of Pisces.

Planets in the Same Sign But Not Conjunct

Two planets in the same sign, but far away from each other by degree, will still operate harmoniously because they share the same

Chart Comparison Form

	Your Planets Degree & Sign	Other's Planets Degree & Sign
Planets		
Sun		
Moon		
Mercury		
Venus		
Mars		
Jupiter		
Saturn		
Uranus		
Neptune		
Pluto		
Angles		
Asc.		
Desc.		
Mc		
Ic		

sign characteristics, but to be felt really strongly, they should be close in orb. For instance, Burton has Uranus at 21 degrees of Pisces. Taylor has Mars at 2 degrees of Pisces. The distance between the two planets, thus, is 19 degrees, pretty far apart for a valid conjunction. But there is still something in common because they share the same sign. Mars conjunct Uranus denotes a fascination that flares up suddenly, but may lead to an unstable relationship. Although we can see that this applies to this couple, there are other closer aspects that will show this also.

Trines And Sextiles

To discover the signs which are trine or sextile to each other is also not difficult. Trines are 120 degrees apart with an orb of about 8 degrees on each side. Sextiles are 60 degrees apart with an orb of about 3 degrees on each side. The following list shows signs that are in harmonious trine or sextile to each other.

Signs	Trines	Sextiles
Aries	Leo, Sagittarius	Aquarius, Gemini
Taurus	Virgo, Capricorn	Pisces, Cancer
Gemini	Libra, Aquarius	Aries, Leo
Cancer	Scorpio, Pisces	Taurus, Virgo
Leo	Sagittarius, Aries	Gemini, Libra
Virgo	Taurus, Capricorn	Cancer, Scorpio
Libra	Gemini, Aquarius	Leo, Sagittarius
Scorpio	Cancer, Pisces	Virgo, Capricorn
Sagittarius	Aries, Leo	Libra, Aquarius
Capricorn	Taurus, Virgo	Scorpio, Pisces
Aquarius	Gemini, Libra	Sagittarius, Aries
Pisces	Cancer, Scorpio	Capricorn, Taurus

Here's an example of how to use this table. If your Sun is at 15 degrees of Aries, any planet in your partner's chart near 15 degrees of Leo or Sagittarius would be trine. (An orb of 8 degrees on either side of 15 would include any planet from 7 to 23 degrees of Leo or Sagittarius.)

To look for sextiles to 15 degrees of Aries, check a mate's chart for any planets at around 15 degrees of Aquarius or Gemini. (An orb of 3 degrees on each side would mean any planet between 12 and 18 degrees of Aquarius or Gemini.) Again, these orbs may extend over into the preceding or following sign, just as explained above for a conjunction. Burton's Mars at 28 degrees of Libra has an orb of 8 degrees for a trine. That would take it up to 6 degrees of Scorpio. On the table above, you'll see that Scorpio is trine

Pisces. Taylor has Mars at 2 degrees of Pisces. Thus Burton's Mars is trine Taylor's Mars.

Squares And Oppositions

To discover the signs that are square or opposed each other is just as simple. Squares are 90 degrees apart with an orb of about 10 degrees on each side. Oppositions are 180 degrees apart with a similar orb. The following list shows signs that are in challenging square or opposition to each other

Signs	Squares	Oppositions
Aries	Cancer, Capricorn	Libra
Taurus	Leo, Aquarius	Scorpio
Gemini	Virgo, Pisces	Sagittarius
Cancer	Libra, Aries	Capricorn
Leo	Scorpio, Taurus	Aquarius
Virgo	Sagittarius, Gemini	Pisces
Libra	Capricorn, Cancer	Aries
Scorpio	Aquarius, Leo	Taurus
Sagittarius	Pisces, Virgo	Gemini
Capricorn	Aries, Libra	Cancer
Aquarius	Taurus, Scorpio	Leo
Pisces	Gemini, Sagittarius	Virgo

71

Again, if your Sun is at 15 degrees of Aries, any planet within 10 degrees orb of 15 degrees of Cancer or Capricorn is square to it, while a mate's planet in orb of 15 degrees of Libra would be in opposition. Here, too, if you have a planet at a late or early degree of a sign, you should allow the orb, in this case 10 degrees, even if it stretches over into the preceding or following sign.

A Word about Orbs of Distance

Although astrologers often disagree on the number of degrees that constitute a valid orb, the orbs I recommend above for chart comparison are fairly generous. Once again, I suggest you use 10 degrees on either side for the conjunction, square, or opposition, 8 degrees for a trine, and 3 degrees for a sextile. Naturally, the closer the orb, the stronger the effect of the aspect will be.

Sorting The Aspects

To make a comparison simpler, you would then sort the aspects into favorable or challenging ones. Here's how I would proceed with Burton and Taylor's comparison. I would list the trines and sextiles in one column and the squares and oppositions in another. The conjunctions can be either favorable or challenging depending upon the planets involved. (See the list on page 74 for this information.) In each case, Burton's planet will be listed first.

72

Favorable Aspects	Challenging Aspects
Sun trine Sun	Sun square Jupiter
Sun conjunct Moon	Moon opposition Sun
Sun trine Pluto	Moon opposition Mercury
Moon conjunct Neptune	Moon opposition Mars
Moon sextile MC	Mercury square Sun
Mercury sextile Ascendant	Mercury square Mercury
Venus sextile Sun	Mercury square Mars
Venus sextile Mercury	Mercury square Neptune
Venus sextile Mars	Venus square Ascendant
Venus trine Neptune	Mars square Saturn
Venus conjunct IC	Venus square Jupiter
Mars trine Mars	Jupiter square Uranus
Saturn trine Sun	Jupiter opposite Pluto
Saturn trine Pluto	Saturn square Jupiter
Uranus trine Moon	Uranus square Uranus
Uranus trine Pluto	Neptune square Moon
Neptune trine Venus	Pluto square Venus
Neptune trine Uranus	Pluto square Uranus
Ascendant conjunct Pluto	Ascendant square Venus

Favorable Aspects (cont.)
  MC conjunct Sun
  MC conjunct Mercury

Challenging Aspects
  Ascendant square Uranus

What Their Aspects Spelled Out

As you can see, in the case of Burton and Taylor, the lists of favorable and challenging are fairly even. There are almost as many challenging aspects as harmonious ones. This often points to a difficult relationship. There is a great deal to draw them together. They had all the basic requirements of the four love planets, Sun, Moon, Venus, and Mars. But there is just as much to cause conflict and pull them apart. His Moon and Mercury in Virgo and Sagittarius, for instance, made harsh aspects to her romantic Pisces planets. Ideas about home life and communication were the problems here. They often hurt each other with angry words and misunderstandings, no matter how great the attraction and how much they sincerely loved each other.

If you look at their charts on pages 157–8, you'll see the major problems graphically displayed. His critical, hard-to-please Moon in Virgo opposed her Pisces planets, giving him different ideas about lifestyles. In addition, his outspoken Mercury in Sagittarius squared her Pisces Mars. This is an argument aspect par excellence. He often told it like he saw it, very directly, and she fought back from wounded feelings.

Other Relationship Examples

An Ideal Relationship

The greater the ratio of good aspects to challenging ones, the more chance a relationship has to endure. You may need a few squares and oppositions to add spice and variety, but the happiest, long-lasting partnership will have many more good aspects than negative. I've seen some with as many as twenty-seven favorable aspects against three negative ones.

Favorable Conjunctions in Chart Comparisons

Sun/Moon	Moon/Neptune	Mars/Jupiter
Sun/Mercury	Mercury/Mercury	Jupiter/Jupiter
Sun/Venus	Mercury/Venus	Jupiter/Uranus
Sun/Jupiter	Mercury/Jupiter	Jupiter/Neptune
Moon/Moon	Mercury/Uranus	Uranus/Uranus
Moon/Mercury	Venus/Venus	Uranus/Neptune
Moon/Venus	Venus/Mars	Neptune/Neptune
Moon/Mars	Venus/Jupiter	Pluto/Pluto
Moon/Jupiter		

74

Challenging Conjunctions in Chart Comparison

Sun/Saturn	Venus/Saturn	Saturn/Neptune
Moon/Saturn	Mars/Saturn	Saturn/Pluto
Mercury/Saturn	Mars/Pluto	

Note: The categories of other conjunctions depend on how well they are aspected in the respective natal charts or between charts.

Favorable or Challenging Conjunctions

A Friendship Only

If you have many good aspects, however, and they do not include the vital love planet connections, you may have a wonderful friendship, but not a real love connection. This is especially true in the cases of couples whose comparisons don't include the aspects that indicate strong sexual compatibility. Here is a good example of that in the charts of the Prince and Princess of Wales, Charles and Diana, who have recently separated.

	Charles' Planets Degree & Sign	**Diana's Planets** Degree & Sign
Planets		
Sun	22° Scorpio	9° Cancer
Moon	0° Taurus	25° Aquarius
Mercury	6° Scorpio	3° Cancer
Venus	16° Libra	24° Taurus
Mars	20° Sagittarius	1° Virgo
Jupiter	29° Sagittarius	5° Aquarius
Saturn	5° Virgo	27° Capricorn
Uranus	29° Gemini	23° Leo
Neptune	14° Libra	8° Scorpio
Pluto	16° Leo	6° Virgo
Angles		
Asc.	5° Leo	18° Sagittarius
Desc.	5° Aquarius	18° Gemini
MC	13° Aries	18° Virgo
IC	13° Libra	18° Pisces

Favorable Aspects	**Challenging Aspects**
Sun trine Sun (by sign)	Sun square Moon
Sun sextile Saturn	Sun opposite Venus
Moon sextile Mercury	Sun square Uranus
Moon trine Mars	Mercury square Jupiter
Moon trine Pluto	Mercury square Saturn
Mercury trine Sun	Venus square Sun
Mercury trine Mercury	Mars square MC/IC
Mercury conjunct Neptune	Jupiter opposite Sun
Mercury sextile Pluto	Jupiter opposite Mercury
Mars trine Uranus	Saturn conjunct Mars
Mars conjunct Ascendant	Saturn conjunct Pluto
Jupiter trine Mars	Neptune square Sun

Favorable Aspects (cont.)

Jupiter trine Uranus

Saturn sextile Mercury

Saturn sextile Neptune

Uranus conjunct Sun

Uranus trine Moon

Uranus conjunct Mercury

Uranus sextile Mars

Neptune trine Jupiter

Pluto trine Asc./sextile Desc.

Descendant conjunct Jupiter

MC trine Ascendant

IC trine Descendant

Challenging Aspects

Pluto square Venus

Pluto conjunct Uranus

Pluto square Neptune

Ascendant opposite Jupiter

Asc./Desc. square Neptune

MC/IC square Sun

MC/IC square Mercury

76

Why Charles and Diana Didn't Get Along

As you can see from the above list, there were many obstacles and challenges for these two. Again, as with Burton and Taylor, there are almost as many challenging aspects as favorable ones, but this is much less the passionate affair. It was one based on good communication and excitement at the beginning of their relationship, but not much else later on.

There is little real love lost here because there are just no good Venus aspects between the two charts. They would definitely like different kinds of social life, ruled by Venus. She has only one good aspect to his Sun, representing his masculinity, and three adverse aspects. The one good aspect is made by Saturn, planet of duty and responsibility.

They were right for each other by Sun sign, both being compatible water signs, Scorpio and Cancer, trine to each other. However, there was no favorable Mars/Venus link to indicate strong sexual attraction. Nor are there Venus/Pluto links or Venus/ Uranus aspects between charts to show the kind of excitement and attraction needed between the sexes. His Sun is square her Uranus. This could have produced initial attraction, but with squares from Uranus, the attraction is usually not long-lasting. Her Sun is widely conjunct his Uranus (from 29 degrees of Gemini to 9 degrees of Cancer), which also spells temporary attraction.

A Harmonious Relationship

The best example I've found to date of a truly harmonious relationship was between two people who lived together, but never married. They were William Randolph Hearst and his long-time mistress, actress Marion Davies. You'll read more about them in Chapter Six, "Determining Mutual Money Luck," but just so you can see a good example of harmony between charts here are their planets and aspects.

	Hearst's Planets Degree & Sign	Davies' Planets Degree & Sign
Planets		
Sun	8° Taurus	13° Capricorn
Moon	17° Virgo	16° Capricorn
Mercury	18° Taurus	2° Aquarius
Venus	11° Gemini	25° Aquarius
Mars	0° Cancer	12° Gemini
Jupiter	20° Libra	10° Virgo
Saturn	29° Virgo	27° Scorpio
Uranus	18° Gemini	27° Scorpio
Neptune	4° Aries	18° Gemini
Pluto	10° Taurus	12° Gemini
Angles		
Asc.	23° Taurus	23° Sagittarius
Desc.	23° Scorpio	23° Gemini
MC	4° Aquarius	15° Libra
IC	4° Leo	15° Aries

Favorable Aspects	**Challenging Aspects**
Sun trine Sun	Sun square Mercury
Sun trine Moon	Moon square Neptune

Favorable Aspects (cont.)

Sun trine Jupiter
Moon trine Moon
Mercury trine Sun
Mercury trine Moon
Venus conjunct Mars
Venus conjunct Neptune
Venus conjunct Pluto
Venus trine MC
Mars trine Venus
Jupiter trine Venus
Jupiter trine Neptune
Jupiter sextile Ascendant
Jupiter conjunct MC
Saturn trine Mercury
Saturn sextile Saturn
Saturn sextile Uranus
Uranus conjunct Neptune
Uranus trine Ascendant
Uranus trine MC
Neptune sextile Mercury
Pluto trine Sun
Pluto trine Jupiter
MC conjunct Mercury

Challenging Aspects

Venus square Jupiter
Jupiter square Moon
Ascendant square Venus
Ascendant opposite Saturn
Ascendant opposite Uranus

78

Here you have many more favorable aspects than challenging, but even most of the challenging aspects above are between benefic planets that are not really very challenging. The squares involving Moon, Venus, and Jupiter would be more likely to indicate a relationship in which one party spoils the other than to real differences of opinion. Only her Saturn and Uranus in his seventh house of marriage, opposing his Ascendant, had a really adverse effect. It probably helped prevent a legitimate union in their case.

In further chapters, we'll examine other factors which I have found important in comparing charts. You might share good Sun/Moon and Venus/Mars ties with a member of the opposite sex, for example, but for the magic that results in a vital union, some more subtle connections may be needed. Indeed, some of these more subtle ties may bring people together even when their charts don't aspect each other perfectly.

In Chapter Nine, we'll examine the Sun/Moon midpoint and how it must make an important aspect to the other's chart for marriage to result. In Chapter Ten, you'll see how Arabic parts and karmic ties can tell you if a partner is really right for you. Chapter Six will show you how to compare charts to see if both of you will benefit financially from the union.

Chapter Six

Determining Mutual Money Luck

I assume that if you are reading this book you wish to marry for more than money. Even if love is uppermost on your mind, however, money is bound to be important. If you wed someone whose planets afflict the money-making or money-receiving aspects shown in your chart, happiness may be difficult to sustain.

The truth is some people will be extremely fortunate for you financially, others moderately so, and others may handicap you in what you do. To some extent, these tendencies will, of course, be shown in your own chart. Look at the relationships between your own seventh house of partners and eighth house of partner's earning ability to see what is promised.

If, for instance, you have Saturn, the planet of limitations in your eighth house, and it is square the ruler of your seventh, then you might expect that partners will be of little help to you in the financial department. If there are

both good and bad aspects, however, you have a better chance. You can choose someone whose money planets may bring out the best in your chart financially.

Here's an example: You might have a semisquare between a planet in the seventh and one in the eighth, but could at the same time have a trine between the rulers of the two houses. By all means, look for a partner whose Jupiter, Venus, and trines smile fortunately on that trine of yours. Be wary of persons whose planets emphasize your semisquare. Remember, you can enhance your own earning prospects and those of your partner if you use astrology wisely.

Timing is important. When you set your wedding date, when you make large purchases, or any other joint financial decisions, do so when the planets are in good aspect to both charts money-wise. Much more important will be the permanently favorable aspects from the chart of a lover, colleague, or partner who turns your chart into a money-making winner.

What Makes for Money Power?

Whether your own chart is good, bad, or medium in regard to money, remember that the right partner will help. A poor money chart can be bolstered while an excellent one can be made even more fortunate by influences from the other's horoscope.

Here's how to recognize a poor money chart. Obstacles to *earning money* will be shown primarily by lack of planetary power connected with the second house of income and possessions. For example, suppose one has no planets in the second house. That is not necessarily bad, but then suppose that the ruling planet of the sign on the cusp of the second is very weak. It might be obscured behind the scenes in the twelfth house, its only aspects a conjunction to Saturn, the planet of limitations, and a square to Uranus.

The above describes the chart of poet John Keats, who achieved fame after his death, but whose earning powers during his brief life were practically nil. Uranus, ruling his midheaven of fame, however, was making good aspects to his Sun, Neptune, and Venus of poetry in his sixth house of work. Keats never married; he died of tuberculosis at age 26. If he had married, he might have been more fortunate if his partner's money planets made up for the lack of money luck in his chart.

There are many other examples of charts that might show real promise in one area of life, but not in money. You might, for instance, have a chart with the ruler of the second in the sixth of hard work, its only aspects a square to Neptune or an opposition to Uranus. Your dreams of money through your work might never really be realized with such aspects.

Even if you have one of these very low money-making charts, you don't have to necessarily marry to improve your income. You could help yourself by working with or for someone whose planets add power to your weak second house. On the other hand, if you have a strong eighth house—ruling inheritance, gifts, windfalls, or spousal support—you might not need a spectacular second house.

The ideal money chart would contain well-aspected planets in both second and eighth houses, plus lucky sextiles and trines or positive conjunctions to the rulers of these houses, but even such a chart could be improved by the right partner.

Assess Your Own Money Power

First, find your own "money planets." These are the ones that fall in your second house of earning or in your eighth house of joint finances and inheritances, gifts, and such. You can still be prosperous without planets in these houses, but they do help to center attention on financial affairs.

Next, look at the planets that rule the signs on the cusps of these houses. Include rulers of intercepted signs in these houses also. The signs and houses and aspects these planets make will tell the story of your financial fortune.

The Moon's Nodes in the second or eighth houses can also be considered to center attention on money and possessions. So will planets anywhere in your chart in the money signs of Taurus and Scorpio. If Jupiter or Venus are well-aspected in your money houses, you are doubly blessed.

If you are interested in making money through speculative ventures, then also consider the condition of your fifth house, since this house and its rulers governs how lucky you will be in taking a chance in improving your finances.

Next, it may be helpful to circle the "money planets" in your chart. Then draw lines to each planet they aspect. If they are mainly unaspected by other planets, they possess less power. If this is the case in your chart, you need to find someone whose chart makes up for this with trines and sextiles to your money planets, or perhaps a fortunate Jupiter conjunction.

Perhaps your "money planets" are heavily aspected, but mostly with squares and oppositions. It's true that a T-square can add drive and dynamic action to your life, but too many such aspects might be discouraging. To make it all easier, ally yourself with a partner whose planets add one or more trines or sextiles.

If you discover both favorable and challenging aspects to your money planets, but mostly good, you'll fall into the category that most very successful people do. When there is enough luck indicated by trines and sextiles, then the squares have the potential to add drive and a sense of competition that will push you forward.

You still can increase your good fortune by marrying someone whose money planets fill out the third points to any "money trines" you may have. Such a mate will not only increase your good fortune, but will also be rewarded through the "grand money trine" that results.

Here's an example: Your Sun in your second house is trine your Jupiter in your sixth house. That's good money luck through your work right there. But if your mate has a planet that falls into your tenth house, trine both your Sun and Jupiter, that will increase your good luck and help you receive recognition for your good work and prosperity.

Suppose your second house is far luckier than your eighth. Then you'd be far better at earning money than in receiving spousal support, inheritances, or in joint finances. In such a case, you'd do better not to count too much on the support of another. Suppose your mate's Jupiter falls in your eighth house, or some other lucky aspect. That might change the picture quite a bit.

If your eighth house is luckier than your second, and it's easier for you to acquire money through support from others, you still might like to earn your own money to enhance a feeling of self-worth. Then look for a partner whose Jupiter falls on your second-house ruler or whose other planets make favorable aspects to it.

A Real-Life Case of Fabulous Mutual Money Luck

The best possible scenario between charts of a lucky couple is this; Both have lucky trines to both money houses in their own charts. Then the "money planets" in each chart just happen to supplement and fill out "grand money trines" to the partner's money trines. Will this bring money luck? You bet!

It brought so much money luck to a famous couple of the past that people today still pay hefty prices to tour the castle and possessions that these two amassed together. Although they were never legally married, their charts together were fantastic, especially in the financial department.

In fact, the horoscopes of newspaper magnate William Randolph Hearst and his long-time mistress Marion Davies show that it was not only she who benefitted by their long union. They were mutually beneficial. I have rarely seen such good money luck between charts.

Here were the ingredients: Mercury and Mars ruled his second house of earning. In the second house was dynamic Mars which often lends energy to money-making. On the cusp of the second house was the sign Gemini, which rules newspapers, showing the source of his income. The ruler of Gemini, the planet Mercury, was in his twelfth house and in the money sign, Taurus. His money-luck was not absolute; he had both fortunate and challenging aspects to these planets. On the luck side, Mercury, which rules communication, was trined by the Moon in his fifth house of entertainment and speculation. The Moon enabled him to understand popular tastes (ruled by the Moon) in the area of fast-breaking news items (Mercury).

Even the challenging aspects to his earning planets were not against him, however. Although Mars in the second house received only squares, it was the focal point of a T-square that gave it great power. It drove him to make money aggressively and, according to some stories, even a bit ruthlessly. It also made him a big spender, since Mars rules impulse.

Actress Marion Davies might not have had the luck to become Mrs. Hearst, but she had incredibly fortunate money aspects both from and to Hearst's chart. There is no married couple in my files who had such mutual money luck. Her Sun and Moon in Capricorn filled out the third point of a grand trine to his second house ruler, Mercury.

The grand trine formed between their charts was doubly lucky. Since Virgo was on the cusp of his fifth house of speculation, Mercury also ruled this money house. This meant the grand trine from his Mercury in Taurus to his Moon in Virgo (in the fifth) to Davies' Sun and Moon in Capricorn was lucky for fifth house matters as well. The fifth house, which also rules romance and entertainment, was significant in the way they lived and the grand style in which they entertained.

Hearst's eighth house was also helped by Davies' planets. He had Sagittarius on the cusp, with Jupiter in his sixth house of work, in the sign Libra. This meant fortune in his work through financial partnerships. Jupiter was trine his natal Uranus in Gemini in his first house of personal endeavors. Since Uranus ruled his Midheaven (career), this aspect was very good for recognition and success in his career.

To turn this eighth-house trine into a grand trine, he needed a partner with a strong planet in Aquarius, forming the third point of a lucky money grand trine. To the good fortune of both, Marion Davies had both North Node and Venus in Aquarius, completing this second grand trine.

The Benefits Went Both Ways

As you may have concluded, Davies had a better eighth house than second. Most mistresses and wives of wealthy men do. The eighth, remember, rules support by others, generosity, gifts, inheritances, and windfalls. Although she had a career as an actress, it was sponsored by Hearst. Her money luck actually came more through her alliance with him than from money she earned herself.

The fact is that her horoscope indicates she would be a prime example of one who would gain spectacularly through other people's money and good will. Jupiter, the planet of good luck was in her eighth house. This placement of Jupiter is seen frequently in the charts of heirs and heiresses, winners of contests, or those who marry well.

The Moon and the Sun co-ruled her eighth house since Cancer was on the cusp, and Leo was intercepted there. Both her Sun and Moon were conjoined in the sign Capricorn in the first house of her chart. This indicated her personality, face, and figure would be her fortune, and that fortune would come through others. And since both Sun and Moon were trine Jupiter in the eighth house, it would be a spectacular kind of fortune. As if that weren't enough, Hearst's money planets made this aspect even more powerful. His Sun and Pluto in Taurus, the money sign, filled out the third point of a grand money trine.

Her second house was not bad either. Anyone who had access to so many beautiful possessions would have had a fairly good second house. The art and beauty surrounding her suggest the planet Venus. She did have Venus, and also the lucky North Node and Mercury of communication, in her second house.

The unhappy side of her life was suggested by the square from Venus to both Saturn and Uranus in Scorpio in her eleventh house of hopes and wishes. This suggested not only the great age difference between them—she was a teen-ager and he in his fifties when they met—but the fact that her hopes and wishes about love were frustrated.

Offsetting this difficult aspect, however, was the money grand trine that Hearst's financial planets formed to her Venus in the second house. It seems to show that her money luck came through him. It meant that he was lucky for her in her show business career. He used his resources and his media influence to promote her acting career.

This was an exceptional example of money luck between two charts, indeed. Attesting to the fact that the good luck went both ways is the fact that when he was temporarily down on his luck during the 1930s depression, she was said to have helped him get back on his feet with money she had saved.

Extravagance That Changed the World

Your money planets may help another only too well in some cases. The charts of King Louis XVI of France and his Queen, Marie Antoinette, display extreme examples of too much good luck and a display of wealth that ended in disaster. Conditions in France that led to revolution and the end of the monarchy can be traced to the extravagances of the French court under these two.

Marie Antoinette was not realistic about money or values, as can be seen by Neptune in Leo in her second house of possessions. Neptune is the planet that often results in not seeing conditions clearly, while Leo loves showy display. Neptune ruled her tenth house of reputation. Her reputation with the people was not very good. Mercury rules speech and Sagittarius rules blunt remarks with little thought of their effect.

If the Queen really did say of the people who shouted for bread, "Let them eat cake," such a remark would have come from this aspect. It was so easy for her to fulfill her desires that she didn't think much about their wants or needs. Since Mercury ruled her fourth house of the home and family, she was able to live in a palace that was unequalled for its grandeur, and that wealth came from family, not from her own efforts.

The cusp of the eighth house of other people's money in the King's chart filled out a grand trine to the Queen's Neptune trine Mercury. This influenced him to go along with her luxuries. In addition, her Jupiter, planet of abundance, was in Libra, making good aspects to her money planets. It occupied her fifth house of entertainment and romance. So she could have been very charming and disarming.

More importantly, her Jupiter in Libra fell right into his second house of money, directly on his Venus in Libra. So she must certainly have led him into greater extravagance and spending. However, the spending had to come to an end. Her own eighth house contained and was ruled by the planet Saturn, planet of limitations. True, his Mars in Virgo, ruler of his eighth house, trined her Saturn in Capricorn, ruler of her eighth house. In her own chart her Ascendant and second-house ruler, the Moon, in the fifth house of pleasure, was squared by that Saturn of limitations in her eighth. That was the aspect that led to her downfall and execution since the eighth house can represent death and transformation as well as other people's money. The other people, the populace, finally said "no."

A Case of Non-support

There are an infinite amount of possible money patterns between the charts of two people. Sometimes only one planet can make a big difference. One man had his Uranus right on the eighth house cusp of his partner. The unpredictable planet, Uranus can often indicate a complete turn-around of what is expected. He expected to make a great deal of money and support her in grand style, but the combination of their money planets favored her second house and his eighth house.

None of her planets aspected his second house well, but her second-house ruler was trine his eighth-house ruler, Saturn. When he could not seem to earn a living after they were married, she supported him for several years from a sense of duty (Saturn). None of her planets made any good aspects to his second house ruler, so his efforts at money-making all seemed to fail. Both his Sun and Saturn trined her second-house ruler, so she was able to support them both, although at low-paying Saturnian jobs. A square from his Pluto to her second-house ruler also caused her to feel manipulated and pressured into working rather than raising a family. This marriage failed finally after five years because of mutual frustrations.

A Case of Ample Support

As in the preceding case, often a planet exactly conjunct your second or eighth ruler or cusp will tell the story. One man, who has made a great deal of money, has his Sun directly on his wife's eighth-house ruler. But his Moon squares her second house ruler. Thus, she is much more fortunate through him when he makes the money. In turn, *her* Sun is conjunct his second house cusp. So she encourages him to earn.

A Case of Mutual Supportiveness

Another man has his Jupiter conjunct his wife's second-house ruler. Her income immediately went up after their marriage. Her Mercury conjuncts his second-house ruler, so she helps stimulate him to think about ways to increase his earnings.

What Some of the Aspects Indicate

As you can see above, conjunctions of one person's planets with the other's money rulers are very powerful, and, as I have said, trines and sextiles are very helpful also. An opposition between money rulers might indicate differences about how to earn money. A square between money rulers may indicate obstacles to be overcome. A husband could object to a wife's career or one spouse might push the other into uncongenial work.

The quincunx is particularly interesting. If your second-house ruler is quincunx (150 degrees) your partner's second-house ruler, you may find yourself making adjustments in the way you earn a living after you're married. You might lose a job or quit it, or be forced into an entirely new career. It may call for constant financial adjustments. One couple who has this aspect between rulers of their eighth houses are doing well, but are constantly refinancing loans in order to get ahead.

Some General Planetary Observations

Sun — If one of your money planets is the Sun, pride and self-worth are connected to your ability to make money. With a weak or blocked Sun, you may constantly feel frustrated by a lack of prowess at proving yourself financially. Another's Sun to a money planet of yours will indicate a person whose ego is involved in making you look good. They'll help through personality and vitality. With adverse aspects to your money planet, the Sun might indicate some competition with you.

Moon — With the Moon as one of your money planets, you are very emotional about money, earning, and spending. You go by your feelings and intuition in money affairs. Security will always seem very important. Another's Moon in aspect will provide a person who empathizes and understands where you are coming from financially. Adversely aspected from another's chart, the Moon might cause some emotional turmoil over financial decisions.

Mercury — You will be more mental and rational about money with Mercury as one of your money planets. You'll think about and talk about money, and could gain through communication fields. There's a chance you could be very shrewd, changeable, or even unreliable in money dealings, depending on aspects. Another's Mercury favorable to yours stimulates your thinking about ways to make money. A mate might provide good financial advice and would be someone who's always ready to listen with interest to your money ideas. With an unfavorable Mercury aspect from a mate, you might find yourself being criticized or talked into, or out of, money plans.

Venus — A Venus money planet can make you extravagant, but pleasant and generous in financial matters. You'll want to follow your heart in earnings and can be successful through art, beauty, music, diplomacy, or entertainment. If your own Venus is adversely aspected, you might be a spendthrift or lazy. Another's Venus, favorable to your money planets, grants favors, approves, and aids you to gain through social activities. Another's Venus, adverse to your money planets, might indicate lack of approval or pettiness in financial dealings.

Mars — With Mars as a money planet, you'll be energetic about earning and will possess great drive and financial ambition. Adversely aspected, your Mars could also indicate you would be overly reckless, aggressive, ruthless, or competitive. Another's Mars, favorable, provides someone who'll be active and ardent in supporting your aims. Another's Mars, adverse to your money planets, means challenge or competition or outright blocking of your financial interests.

Jupiter — Jupiter as a money planet is very lucky. You will be optimistic, generous, and upbeat about money, usually leading to big success. Or, if squared or opposed in your chart, it might make you too extravagant and unrealistic about earning and spending.

Another's Jupiter, favorable to your money planets, is a Santa Claus aspect. You'll be encouraged and treated quite generously by your mate. If adverse, another's Jupiter can encourage you to over-do in some way in financial affairs.

Saturn — With Saturn as one of your money planets, you may be more security-conscious about money. You'll work hard, some-times feel as if you never have enough—no matter how rich you are—and may be quite responsible and mature about financial affairs. Or you might feel so fearful and restricted that you never think big enough to make big money moves. Another's Saturn, favorable, can aid you in organizing efforts and following through in a dutiful way. Another's Saturn, adverse to your money planets, might mean a mate who could frustrate and discourage you, some-one who would not be overly generous with you.

Uranus — Uranus as a money planet means you'll have many orig-inal, inventive ideas about financial affairs. If squared or opposed, it could mean a sporadic income, impulsive spending, or many ups and downs in money matters. Another's Uranus, favorable, might bring unexpected gain; it could mean a mate who'll help you cash in on good ideas. Adversely aspected to your money planets, anoth-er's Uranus could mean reverses, unexpected events, or a less than steady flow of income.

Neptune — When Neptune is a money planet, you may benefit through inspiration, artistic and musical talents, acting, dancing, diplomacy, or the entertainment business. Or, adversely, you may be unrealistic, confused, deceptive, or easily duped. Another's Nep-tune favorable to your money planets can mean someone who believes in you and shows faith and innate understanding of your plans. Adverse aspects from another's Neptune to your money planets could bring someone who is deceptive, tricky, confused, or muddled in financial dealings with you.

Pluto — If Pluto is a money planet, power and resourcefulness can help you deal in high finance. If afflicted, watch obsessiveness about earning, spending, or a need to dominate in money matters.

Another's Pluto, favorable, lends power and support to your financial plans. If adverse to your money planets, another's Pluto could make you feel blocked, subtly dominated, or pressured in earning, spending, or joint financial affairs.

Chapter Seven

When Your Progressed Planets Promise Love or Marriage

Transits can tell you a great deal about your love life, but the year that you walk down the aisle will *always* show up in your progressions. So this is probably the most important chapter in the book, containing the most vital keys to your future prospects.

I always look first for marriage aspects when an unmarried client comes for a reading. I know that sooner or later the question will be asked: "What do you see in my chart about romance or marriage?"

Because I wanted to be highly accurate about this, I've researched the question for some time, setting up the charts of many couples at the time of marriage, and testing all the probable factors. What stands out more than anything else is that there will be from three to ten different progressed "marriage aspects" during the year that the marriage or union takes place.

The stronger the aspects are, the more likely marriage is to take place. You will need some strong "bachelor instincts" to counteract them. If you have significant planets in freedom-loving signs, or a very great need for independence shown by your Uranus placement, you may be more resistant to marriage than others.

Then, too, remember the old adage that nothing happens that is not shown in the natal chart. Difficult aspects to the ruler of your seventh house, for example, may mean difficulty in finding the right partner. Also, conflicts in your chart between the signs of your Sun, Moon, Venus, and Mars can also result in conflicts in making the decision to march to the altar.

If you feel ready for marriage, ready for commitment with the right person, you should definitely examine your progressed chart to see if the planets are on your side. It's very simple to spot marriage aspects. Once again, they involve Sun, Moon, Venus, and Mars, plus the ruler of the seventh house or planets in the seventh house.

A Word About Progressions

For determining the most likely years for marriage, I use the system of prediction called secondary progressions. In this most common way of progressing a natal chart, each day after birth represents a year of your life. I also use converse directions; not only do the planetary positions on the days after birth relate to life events, but so do the days before birth.

Although many astrologers have not discovered the strength and validity of converse directions, I follow the example of the late

R.C. Davison, who outlined the system in his excellent book, *The Technique of Prediction.*

It was his opinion that converse directions were more karmic in nature and more involved with forces set into motion through the exercise of free will in past incarnations. He felt that secondary progressions, based on the days after birth, were more amenable to our modification through current free will.

I find that the interplay of aspects between natal chart, secondary progressions, and converse directions will show most effectively the strength of marriage probability for any particular year. Setting these directions around the natal chart will tell the story best. It is here that three to ten strong aspects will usually show up during a marriage year.

I'll give you more concrete examples of how I do this later in the chapter. First, I want to give you some simple techniques that may help to spot marriage years at a glance, first from a look at the natal chart and, secondly, from a glance at the ephemeris of the year you were born.

Marriage Years in the Natal Chart

Sometimes your marriage year will show up very plainly in your natal chart. It involves the distances between your love planets, angles, and, sometimes, the Part of Marriage. Here are a few examples of how it works.

First, you can count the number of degrees between the love planets (Sun, Moon, Venus, and Mars) and the angles (Ascendant, Descendant, Midheaven, and IC). An astrologer glancing at Elizabeth Taylor's chart at birth would have seen many marriages probable. Her most recent marriage, at age 58, to Larry Fortensky, shows up quite plainly in this way. Mars and the IC are involved, as they often are when women marry. A progressed conjunction between these two is one of the most common aspects I have found in women's marriage charts. In Example I (page 98) note that her IC is at 4 degrees of Capricorn. Her Mars is in the fifth house at 2 degrees of Pisces. There are 58 degrees between. Mars is even more important in her chart because it is not only a love planet, but rules the sign of Aries on her seventh house of partners.

Prince Albert, who married Queen Victoria of England when he was 21 years old, has Venus in his twelfth house, only 21 degrees above his Ascendant at 11 degrees of Virgo. See Example II (below). This same age shows up in at least two other places in his natal chart. Neptune is the ruler of his seventh house of partners, and is in his fourth house at 26 degrees of Sagittarius. It is only 21 degrees past his IC. In addition, his Part of Marriage in his seventh house is 21 degrees above his Descendant.

98

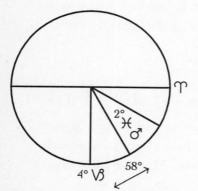

Example I: Elizabeth Taylor
8th marriage — age 58
58 degrees between IC and Mars,
7th house ruler

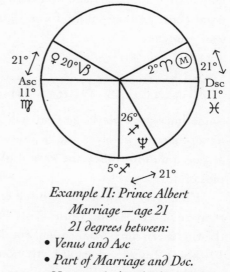

Example II: Prince Albert
Marriage — age 21
21 degrees between:
- *Venus and Asc*
- *Part of Marriage and Dsc.*
- *Neptune (ruler of 7th) and IC*

Note: Love Planets are Sun, Moon, Venus, and Mars, plus 7th house ruler or 7th house planet. Angles are Ascendant (Asc.), Descendant (Desc.), Midheaven (MC), and IC (4th house cusp).

A. Counting Degrees Between Love Planets and Angles

The Part of Marriage often is a vital key to the age at marriage. In Example III (below), this anonymous young lady married at age 21. Note that there are 21 degrees between her Part of Marriage (12 degrees of Scorpio) and her Saturn (3 degrees of Sagittarius). Saturn rules her seventh house Capricorn Descendant. (I'll show you how to figure *your* Part of Marriage in Chapter Ten.)

Poet Percy Bysshe Shelley married at age 22. His Part of Marriage (20 degrees of Cancer) is 22 degrees from his Venus in his fifth house of romance. See Example IV (below).

Sometimes you'll find that by dividing in half the distance between a love planet and an angle, you'll find the correct marriage age. See Example V, Anonymous (page 100). This woman whose Sun is at 20 degrees of Aquarius married at age 26. By that time,

99

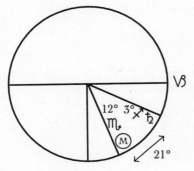

*Example III: Anonymous
Marriage—age 21
21 degrees between Part of
Marriage and 7th ruler*

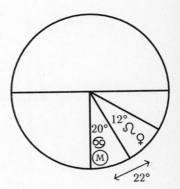

*Example IV: Percy Bysshe Shelley
Marriage—age 22
22 degrees between Part of
Marriage and Venus*

Note: Love Planets are Sun, Moon, Venus, and Mars, plus 7th house ruler or 7th house planet. Angles are Ascendant (Asc.), Descendant (Desc.), Midheaven (MC), and IC (4th house cusp).

B. Counting Degrees Between Part of Marriage and Love Planets (or Angle)

her progressed Sun would have moved forward to 16 degrees of Pisces. Meanwhile, her converse IC would have moved backwards from 12 degrees of Aries to 16 degrees of Pisces, forming a Sun conjunct IC. Examples of this type work especially well when MC, IC, and Sun are involved, because by progression they all move at approximately one degree per year.

Spotting Marriage Years from a Glance at the Ephemeris

An ephemeris usually beats a crystal ball for quick glances that reveal a great deal about your future. Sometimes you can look at a

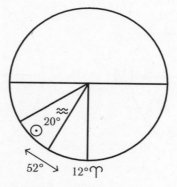

Example V: Anonymous
Marriage — age 26
52 degrees (2 x 26) between
Sun and IC

Note: Love Planets are Sun, Moon, Venus, and Mars, plus 7th house ruler or 7th house planet. Angles are Ascendant (Asc.), Descendant (Desc.), Midheaven (MC), and IC (4th house cusp).

C. Dividing Distance by Half Between Planets and Angles Approaching Each Other —
One by Progression, One by Converse

person's birth page in an ephemeris of planets' places and spot a marriage year just at a glance. You'll probably want to do this, but first, for those of you who are not familiar with how to find progressed aspects quickly, let me add a note of explanation.

Although a computer can tell you your exact progressed aspects for any date, if you have an ephemeris, it's sometimes instructive to look through its pages to see when possible events can take place, especially an event such as marriage.

We'll be concerned only with secondary directions, not converse directions right here, to make the process simpler. These secondary directions are easy to work with. You won't have to do any intricate mathematics to figure out their approximate positions. You'll find them all listed in an ephemeris for your date of birth and for the several months that immediately follow your birth date. (See the illustration of an ephemeris page on page 102 to see how this works.)

Each day after your birth represents one year of your life. It's that simple. If you were born on January 1 of any year, the positions of the Sun, Moon, and planets for that date would comprise your approximate natal chart positions.

The position of these same heavenly bodies for January 2 would represent age one. January 3 would symbolize age two, and so forth. Just keep counting one day for each year of birth to your present age, and you'll find where your current progressed planets are located by sign and degree.

An Easy Way to Begin

One of the most obvious progressions that you can spot in this way is when the ruler of the sign on your first house (representing you) comes into aspect with the ruler of the sign on your seventh house (representing a partner). If you have Gemini rising, for instance, Mercury is your first-house ruler. The opposite sign on your seventh house cusp will be Sagittarius. Jupiter is the ruler of this sign. (If you need to review the rulers of the signs, look back to page 39.)

AUGUST 1958

LONGITUDE

DAY	SID.TIME	☉	☽	TRUE ☊	☿	♀	♂	♃	♄	♅	♆	♇
1	8 38 21	8 ♌ 43 32	29 ♒ 54 4	25 ♎ R 19.4	4 ♍ 55.4	12 ♋ 21.0	6 ♉ 53.9	24 ♎ 24.9	19 ♐ R 29.9	11 ♌ 46.1	2 ♏ 5.7	1 ♍ 14.1
2	8 42 18	9 40 55	12 ♓ 15 25	25 10.6	5 31.4	13 33.4	7 29.6	24 32.0	19 27.8	11 49.8	2 6.3	1 15.9
3	8 46 15	10 38 20	24 23 11	25 4.4	6 3.5	14 45.8	8 5.1	24 39.1	19 25.9	11 53.5	2 7.0	1 17.8
4	8 50 11	11 35 45	6 ♈ 20 11	25 0.8	6 3.4	15 58.3	8 40.3	24 46.4	19 24.9	11 57.2	2 7.6	1 19.7
5	8 54 8	12 33 12	18 10 15	24 59.3	6 54.9	17 10.8	9 15.3	24 53.9	19 22.2	12 1.0	2 8.3	1 21.6
6	8 58 4	13 30 40	29 58 0	24 D 59.1	7 13.9	18 23.4	9 50.1	25 1.4	19 20.5	12 4.7	2 9.0	1 23.5
7	9 2 1	14 28 10	11 ♉ 48 37	24 R 59.4	7 28.0	19 36.1	10 24.6	25 9.1	19 18.9	12 8.4	2 9.8	1 25.4
8	9 5 57	15 25 40	23 47 31	24 59.0	7 37.3	20 48.8	10 58.9	25 16.9	19 17.3	12 12.1	2 10.6	1 27.4
9	9 9 54	16 23 12	6 ♊ 0 2	24 57.1	7 R 41.4	22 1.5	11 32.9	25 24.9	19 15.9	12 15.8	2 11.4	1 29.3
10	9 13 50	17 20 46	18 31 2	24 53.8	7 40.2	23 14.3	12 6.6	25 32.9	19 14.6	12 19.5	2 12.3	1 31.2
11	9 17 47	18 18 21	1 ♋ 24 21	24 47.6	7 33.6	24 27.2	12 40.1	25 41.1	19 13.3	12 23.2	2 13.1	1 33.2
12	9 21 44	19 15 57	14 42 19	24 39.2	7 21.6	25 40.1	13 13.3	25 49.4	19 12.2	12 26.9	2 14.0	1 35.2
13	9 25 40	20 13 34	28 25 8	24 29.5	7 4.1	26 53.0	13 46.2	25 57.8	19 11.1	12 30.6	2 15.0	1 37.1
14	9 29 37	21 11 13	12 ♌ 30 37	24 19.3	6 41.2	28 6.0	14 18.8	26 6.4	19 10.1	12 34.3	2 16.0	1 39.1
15	9 33 33	22 8 53	26 54 13	24 10.0	6 12.9	29 19.0	14 51.1	26 15.0	19 9.8	12 38.0	2 17.0	1 41.1
→ 16	9 37 30	23 6 34	11 ♍ 29 38	24 2.4	5 39.5	0 ♌ 32.1	15 23.1	26 23.7	19 8.5	12 41.7	2 18.0	1 43.0
17	9 41 26	24 4 17	26 9 45	23 57.2	5 1.4	1 45.2	15 54.7	26 32.6	19 7.8	12 45.3	2 19.0	1 45.0
18	9 45 23	25 2 1	10 ♎ 47 51	23 54.5	4 18.9	2 58.3	16 26.1	26 41.6	19 7.2	12 49.0	2 20.1	1 47.0
19	9 49 19	25 59 45	25 18 27	23 D 53.8	3 32.6	4 11.5	16 57.1	26 50.7	19 6.7	12 52.6	2 21.2	1 49.0
20	9 53 16	26 57 31	9 ♏ 37 48	23 54.3	2 43.3	5 24.8	17 27.8	26 59.8	19 6.3	12 56.3	2 22.4	1 51.0
21	9 57 13	27 55 18	26 43 54	23 R 55.0	1 51.7	6 38.0	17 58.2	27 9.8	19 6.0	12 59.9	2 23.6	1 53.0
22	10 1 9	28 53 6	7 ♐ 36 0	23 54.7	0 58.8	7 51.3	18 28.2	27 18.5	19 5.9	13 3.5	2 24.8	1 55.0
23	10 5 6	29 50 55	21 14 13	23 52.7	0 5.6	9 4.7	18 57.8	27 28.0	19 5.8	13 7.1	2 26.0	1 57.0
24	10 9 2	0 ♍ 48 46	4 ♑ 38 59	23 48.5	29 ♌ 13.1	10 18.1	19 27.1	27 37.6	19 D 5.8	13 10.7	2 27.2	1 59.0
25	10 12 59	1 46 37	17 50 41	23 42.1	28 22.4	11 31.6	19 56.1	27 47.3	19 5.8	13 14.3	2 28.5	2 1.0
26	10 16 55	2 44 30	0 ♒ 49 37	23 34.2	27 34.7	12 45.0	20 24.6	27 57.1	19 6.0	13 17.9	2 29.8	2 2.9
27	10 20 52	3 42 24	18 35 53	23 25.3	26 51.0	13 58.6	20 52.8	28 6.9	19 6.3	13 21.4	2 31.2	2 4.9
28	10 24 48	4 40 20	26 9 36	23 16.6	26 12.2	15 12.1	21 20.6	28 16.9	19 6.7	13 24.9	2 32.5	2 6.9
29	10 28 45	5 38 17	8 ♓ 31 13	23 8.7	25 39.4	16 25.7	21 48.0	28 27.0	19 7.2	13 28.4	2 35.9	2 8.9
30	10 32 42	6 36 16	20 41 28	23 2.5	25 13.3	17 39.4	22 15.0	28 37.1	19 7.8	13 31.9	2 35.3	2 10.9
31	10 36 38	7 ♍ 34 16	2 ♈ 41 49	22 58.3	24 54.5	18 53.1	22 41.6	28 ♎ 47.4	19 ♐ 8.4	13 ♌ 35.4	2 ♏ 36.3	2 ♍ 12.9

SEPTEMBER 1958

LONGITUDE

DAY	SID.TIME	☉	☽	TRUE ☊	☿	♀	♂	♃	♄	♅	♆	♇
1	10 40 35	8 ♍ 32 19	14 ♈ 34 26	22 ♎ 56.1	24 ♌ 43.5	20 ♌ 6.8	23 ♉ 7.8	28 ♎ 57.7	19 ♐ 9.2	13 ♌ 38.9	2 ♏ 38.2	2 ♍ 14.9
2	10 44 31	9 30 23	26 22 17	22 D 55.8	24 D 40.8	21 20.6	23 33.5	29 8.1	19 10.1	13 42.3	2 39.7	2 16.9
3	10 48 28	10 28 29	8 ♉ 9 4	22 56.5	24 46.6	22 34.4	23 58.8	29 18.6	19 11.0	13 45.8	2 41.2	2 18.9
4	10 52 24	11 26 36	19 59 5	22 57.9	25 1.1	23 46.3	24 23.6	29 29.2	19 12.1	13 49.2	2 42.8	2 20.9
5	10 56 21	12 24 46	1 ♊ 57 9	22 59.2	25 24.2	25 2.2	24 48.0	29 39.8	19 13.3	13 52.5	2 44.3	2 22.8
6	11 0 17	13 22 58	14 8 20	22 R 59.6	25 55.8	26 16.1	25 11.9	29 50.6	19 14.5	13 55.9	2 45.9	2 24.8
7	11 4 14	14 21 12	26 37 36	22 56.7	26 35.7	27 30.1	25 35.2	0 ♏ 1.4	19 15.9	13 59.2	2 47.5	2 26.8
8	11 8 10	15 19 28	9 ♋ 29 25	22 56.2	27 23.8	28 44.1	25 58.1	0 12.3	19 17.3	14 2.6	2 49.2	2 28.7
9	11 12 7	16 17 46	22 47 5	22 52.4	28 19.5	29 56.2	26 20.5	0 28.3	19 18.9	14 5.9	2 50.8	2 30.7
10	11 16 4	17 16 6	6 ♌ 32 10	22 47.6	29 22.6	1 ♍ 12.3	26 42.3	0 34.4	19 20.5	14 9.1	2 52.5	2 32.7
11	11 20 0	18 14 28	20 43 52	22 42.5	0 ♍ 32.4	2 26.4	27 3.6	0 45.5	19 22.2	14 12.4	2 54.2	2 34.6
→ 12	11 23 57	19 12 52	5 ♍ 18 34	22 37.7	1 48.5	3 40.6	27 24.3	0 56.7	19 24.1	14 15.6	2 55.9	2 36.5
13	11 27 53	20 11 17	20 10 6	22 33.8	3 10.3	4 54.8	27 44.5	1 8.0	19 26.0	14 18.8	2 57.7	2 38.5
14	11 31 50	21 9 45	5 ♎ 10 21	22 31.3	4 37.2	6 9.0	28 4.1	1 19.3	19 28.0	14 21.9	2 59.4	2 40.4
15	11 35 46	22 8 14	20 10 34	22 D 30.3	6 8.8	7 23.3	28 23.1	1 30.7	19 30.1	14 25.1	3 1.2	2 42.3
16	11 39 43	23 6 46	5 ♏ 2 39	22 30.6	7 44.2	8 37.6	28 41.5	1 42.2	19 32.3	14 28.2	3 3.0	2 44.2
17	11 43 39	24 5 18	19 40 10	22 31.7	9 23.1	9 52.0	28 59.8	1 53.5	19 34.6	14 31.3	3 4.8	2 46.1
18	11 47 36	25 3 53	3 ♐ 58 55	22 32.9	11 4.9	11 6.3	29 16.5	2 5.4	19 37.0	14 34.3	3 6.7	2 48.0
19	11 51 33	26 2 29	17 56 55	22 35.8	12 49.1	12 20.7	29 38.0	2 17.1	19 39.5	14 37.3	3 8.6	2 49.9
20	11 55 29	27 1 7	1 ♑ 33 56	22 R 33.9	14 35.1	13 35.2	29 45.9	2 28.8	19 42.0	14 40.3	3 10.4	2 51.7
21	11 59 26	27 59 47	14 51 4	22 32.5	16 22.7	14 49.6	0 ♊ 4.1	2 40.6	19 44.7	14 43.3	3 12.3	2 53.6
22	12 3 22	28 58 28	27 50 6	22 30.7	18 11.4	16 4.1	0 18.7	2 52.5	19 47.4	14 46.2	3 14.2	2 55.4
23	12 7 19	29 57 11	10 ♒ 33 6	22 27.8	20 0.8	17 18.6	0 32.6	3 4.4	19 50.3	14 49.1	3 16.2	2 57.2
24	12 11 15	0 ♎ 55 56	23 2 20	22 24.4	21 50.7	18 33.2	0 45.7	3 16.8	19 58.2	14 51.9	3 18.1	2 59.1
25	12 15 12	1 54 42	5 ♓ 19 42	22 21.1	23 40.9	19 47.7	0 58.2	3 28.4	19 56.2	14 54.8	3 20.1	3 0.9
26	12 19 8	2 53 30	17 27 9	22 18.2	25 31.1	21 2.3	1 10.0	3 40.4	19 59.8	14 57.6	3 22.1	3 2.7
27	12 23 5	3 52 21	29 26 31	22 16.1	27 21.2	22 16.9	1 21.1	3 52.6	20 2.5	15 0.3	3 24.1	3 4.4
28	12 27 2	4 51 13	11 ♈ 19 37	22 14.9	29 10.9	28 31.6	1 31.4	4 4.7	20 5.8	15 3.0	3 26.1	3 6.2
29	12 30 58	5 50 7	23 8 32	22 D 14.6	1 ♎ 0.3	24 46.3	1 40.9	4 17.0	20 9.1	15 5.7	3 28.1	3 7.9
30	12 34 55	6 ♎ 49 3	4 ♉ 55 34	22 ♎ 15.0	2 ♎ 49.1	26 ♍ 1.0	1 ♊ 49.7	4 ♏ 29.2	20 ♐ 12.6	15 ♌ 8.3	3 ♏ 30.1	3 ♍ 9.7

Madonna was born August 16, 1958. Her Virgo Ascendant is ruled by Mercury. Her 7th house of marriage and partners has Pisces on the cusp; Neptune is the ruler. Look down the page from her birthdate to the place where Mercury and Neptune are first in harmonious aspect to each other by secondary progression. That date is September 12, 1958. This was 27 days after her birthdate. Her marriage to Sean Penn took place when she was 27 years old.

First you would note the placement of your own Mercury and Jupiter at birth. Then you would glance down at the listing of planetary placements in the days after your birth and see when progressed Mercury or progressed Jupiter aspect either these natal places or their progressed places.

You're Never Too Old

One of my favorite stories about this type of ephemeris "quick overviews" concerns the second marriage of a famed Hollywood personality. In early 1979, a young lady of my acquaintance had just run into Fred Astaire on the set of a TV production, talked with him, and had developed a crush on him. This was in spite of the fact that he was almost 80 years old then and she was in her twenties. While visiting with me that evening, she eagerly asked if I knew what was happening to him astrologically at the time. What did the stars proclaim for him?

Since his chart was printed in one of my reference books, I looked at it there, then opened an ephemeris to 1899, the year Astaire was born, to see what his current progressions might be. Since he had been born on May 10, I counted down the page 80 days from that date and came up with July 29, 1899, which would represent 80 years of age for him.

I noted that his progressed Sun that year was at 6 degrees of Leo, trining his natal Uranus. This would indicate surprising events and possibly new interests in his life. But the most obvious favorable progression for the year was between Mercury at 1 degree of Virgo and Jupiter at 1 degree of Scorpio, an exact sextile between the two progressed planets. Jupiter ruled his Sagittarian Ascendant, while Mercury ruled his seventh house of partners in his natal chart.

"Would you believe it," I said, "he has a marriage aspect!"

I glanced back over prior years of his progressed aspects. The last aspect between these two planets had been in 1954 when his wife, Phyllis, had died. At that time Mercury had been square Jupiter, a challenging aspect for partnership in his life. During the years since then he had been single. Now at an advanced age he had a marriage aspect. People had speculated for years why he had not remarried. It was obvious from his progressions that the timing had not been right — until age 80.

A month or so later, these marriage progressions were validated. First the supermarket tabloids reported that Astaire was being seen in public with a young woman jockey named Robyn Smith. They were married not long after that. (Triple-wheel charts for their individual marriage aspects are shown on pages 186–7.)

What the Ephemeris Can Tell You

104　Progressed planets move at different rates, some faster, some much slower. Generally speaking, the five outer planets, Jupiter, Saturn, Uranus, Neptune, and Pluto, don't move very far by progression during the course of a lifetime. So if one of these planets rules your seventh house, look for the faster moving planets — Sun, Moon, Mercury, Venus, and Mars — to make aspects to the slower planets. Since these outer planets are the rulers of Sagittarius, Capricorn, Aquarius, Pisces, or Scorpio, one of these is your seventh house ruler if you have Gemini, Cancer, Leo, Virgo, or Taurus rising. When you look at the ephemeris placements after your birthdate, note when the faster planets move into harmonious alignment with your slower-moving seventh house ruler.

As you glance at the ephemeris, note how much faster the Sun, Moon, Mercury, Venus, or Mars move through the degrees of each sign. If one of these planets rules your seventh house, there is greater chance of them making marriage aspects more often. Since these heavenly bodies are the rulers of Leo, Cancer, Gemini, Virgo, Taurus, Libra, and Aries, one of these is your seventh house ruler if you have Aquarius, Capricorn, Sagittarius, Pisces, Scorpio, Aries, or Libra rising.

With Capricorn rising, however, the progressed Moon that rules your seventh house moves so rapidly — about one degree of a sign per month—that the aspects it makes are not usually considered to be major aspects. Look for aspects to your natal Moon for major marriage-producing aspects.

You'll notice also that the faster-moving Mercury, Venus, and Mars slow way down when they are about to turn retrograde or direct. When they change directions like this (marked by an R or D in your ephemeris), they may move for a while as slowly as the outer planets.

When Madonna Married

If you had been looking in an ephemeris when Madonna first burst upon the national scene, you might have noticed that marriage aspects were coming up for her around age 27. With Virgo rising, this Leo performer had slow-moving Neptune ruling her seventh house of marriage. Neptune was at 2 degrees of Scorpio when she was born on August 16, 1958, and was still at 2 degrees of Scorpio by progression until she married. One of her progressed planets needed to arrive at an aspect to this Neptune for partnership to be a real possibility.

Mercury, ruler of her Virgo ascendant, would have been the perfect planet to make this aspect. Mercury was retrograde at her birth, about to make such an aspect as it moved backward from 5 degrees of Virgo. It connected with a sextile to Neptune when it reached 2 degrees of Virgo when she was around four years of age, hardly old enough for marriage. It continued moving backwards into the sign Leo as she grew, and finally turned direct when she was about 15 or 16. Then Mercury, moving forwards, returned to 2 degrees of Virgo around age 27. She and Sean Penn were married at that time.

As I write this in early 1992, I note that Jupiter is moving forward in Scorpio to conjunct her marriage ruler Neptune. Since both are slow-moving planets, this possible marriage aspect is actually in one-degree orb between ages 28 and 38. Since the seventh-house rules the public as well as partners, it is very probable that the years of this Jupiter conjunct Neptune aspect will represent the peak of her popularity years with the public.

Looking for Marriage Years When a Planet in the Seventh House is Involved

Some people have many more possible marriage years than others do. Elizabeth Taylor is one of these. Not only does Mars rule her seventh house of partners, but both Sun and Uranus are in the seventh house. Thus aspects to all three of these placements can bring marriage aspects.

If *you* have planets in your seventh house, not only will a partnership or marriage be more important to you, but it's possible to have more opportunities for such an alliance. There can be exceptions, however. Fred Astaire, for instance, who went for many years as a single widower, had both Pluto and Neptune in his seventh house. He gained great fame with the public, and had many lovely dancing partners, but he may have been reluctant to marry again after the death of his first wife.

Pluto ruled his twelfth house of secret sorrows. Neptune can be either inspiring or difficult as a seventh-house planet. It rules art, beauty, dancing, films, but also beautiful illusions. Sometimes one with this placement is always looking for the ideal and may not see others as they really are.

In addition, Saturn in his first house opposed this Neptune, creating a high tension between reality and illusion where partners were concerned. When he married for the first time, however, Neptune was aspected very well. There were two good marriage aspects relating to it. His Sun had progressed to 23 degrees of Gemini conjunct natal seventh-house Neptune, plus progressed Neptune had moved forward one degree to 24 Gemini to exactly sextile his natal seventh-house ruler, Mercury, at 24 Aries. His marriage to socialite Phyllis Potter took place in 1933 and was considered to be one of the happiest in Hollywood. That era also coincided with the period when he began a very fortunate series of pictures with dancing partner Ginger Rogers.

Other Marriage Aspects You Can Find in an Ephemeris

There should always be at least one progressed aspect involving the seventh house when marriage takes place. But the back-up aspects will tell the story. As I mentioned earlier, there are usually from three to ten marriage aspects when a wedding occurs. You can look for dates when Venus or Mars are conjunct, trine, or sextile each other, or in the same aspect to Sun or Moon, or when Sun and Moon are in aspect to each other. Or you can find aspects from one of your love planets to your seventh-house ruler.

Do You Currently Have a Marriage Year?

The best way to determine this is to order or run off a triple-wheel computer chart with your natal chart in the inner circle, secondary directions in the middle circle, and converse directions in the outside wheel. (See the illustrations on pages 185–7 to see what this looks like.)

If you don't have a triple-wheel feature on your computer, merely place the current year's progressions, both forward and converse, by hand around the outside of your natal chart. (Or send to a computer service company [see page 151 for a list] for current progressions, both forward and converse, to your natal chart.)

Next, circle all the angles of the three charts with colored pens. There will be twelve of them, four for each chart. Then circle the love planets—Sun, Moon, Venus, and Mars—plus the ruler of your seventh house, and any seventh house planets. Draw lines between any aspects that are formed.

Spot any conjunctions, trines, or sextiles between Sun, Moon, Venus, or Mars. Look also for those very important conjunctions, trines, or sextiles of one or more of these planets to an angle of the chart. These indications may be in the progressed love planets or angles to the natal chart or to the converse chart. Or they may show up in converse angles and love planets to natal or to progressed planets.

The older astrologers claimed that Moon and Venus were the planets to look for in a man's marriage aspects, and that Sun and Mars were indicated in a woman's marriage aspects. This is true to some extent, but does not tell the whole story. In my research, I have found that Sun and Mars conjunctions, or one of these two conjunct the IC, to be found frequently in women's marriage aspects. They can be found also, to a lesser extent, in men's marriage indications.

Whatever else you find, remember that there must be, in addition, a progression involving the seventh house of partners. If Jupiter rules the seventh house, or is in the seventh house, for instance, there could be a progressed or converse direction that involves natal, progressed, or converse Jupiter.

The Most Frequent Combinations in Marriage Aspects

According to my research of charts at the time of marriage, Venus, the planet of love, is most frequently seen in some combination in an individual's progressions or converse directions that year. Next in frequency is the Sun, then Mars, and then the Moon. These are the possible combinations:

Venus / Mars — A conjunction, trine, or sextile between these two brings the enhanced sexual appeal and interest that often leads to marriage. This is one of the most frequent indicators of a marriage year in the charts of both men and women.

Sun / Venus — When these two planets meet by conjunction, trine, or sextile, there is usually a great love in the life. This combination shows up frequently in the marriage aspects of both men and women.

Sun / Mars — For women, this is the third most important marriage indicator. Although there may be other meanings attached to this combination, it is important in many marriage charts. It is frequently the strongest indicator, especially when conjunct. It can be found in a man's marriage chart from time to time, but not as often.

Sun / Moon — This aspect, especially the conjunction, occurs in marriage years, but not nearly as frequently. Since the conjunction shows a New Moon—or new start—in some area of life, it may apply to other activities besides romance and marriage, but since the Sun and Moon relate to male and female energies coming together, it is potentially a marriage or relationship indicator.

Moon / Venus and Moon / Mars — Both of these are far less frequent in marriage aspects, but should be counted as such in backing up stronger indications.

A Question You May Ask

What if you have no marriage planet interchanges such as the preceding—can you still have marriage aspects? The answer is a definite "yes." These combinations are more likely to show up in women's progressions and converse directions than in men's, but a third or more of the female charts had no marriage planet interchange, while more than half of the male charts lacked these aspects. In these cases, the marriage planets were in strong aspect to the all-important angles of the chart.

What's Your Angle on Marriage?

In a triple wheel as described above, with natal chart in the center, and progressed and converse charts for the current year around it, you'll have three sets of four angles (MC, IC, Ascendant, and Descendant). This gives you twelve placements that can make aspects to the four marriage planets in natal, progressed, or converse charts. Plenty of chances, to be sure. It will help to find the marriage planet aspects to angles if you use a colored pen or pencil to circle the degrees of each angle and then put a colored dot beside each marriage planet in each of the three charts. Next, draw a line between the possible conjunctions, trines, and sextiles that are within one degree of orb.

You might think that with all these possibilities everyone would have marriage aspects all the time. This is not the case. I have seen charts go for a number of years without the requisite three to ten such indications. Then, too, the seventh house must be strongly aspected as well to really bring a partnership about.

Differences Between Male and Female Angle Aspects

Conjunctions to the angles are especially important in a marriage year, but the angles aspected seem to differ in importance between men and women as to which is conjoined by a love planet in the year of marriage. The IC, the cusp that rules the fourth house of home and family, has been most frequently found as an indicator of marriage in women's charts. The Midheaven (or MC), ruling one's status in the world, runs a close second. Next comes the Descendant, with aspects to the Ascendant last.

Men, however, are much more inclined to marry with a marriage planet conjunct the Ascendant. Midheaven conjunctions are next for men, then IC, with Descendant least frequent.

When Progressed Planets Promise Love or Marriage

With the changes in the roles of male and female that we are seeing more and more, these statistics may change in the future, but in the charts I studied the preceding rules applied.

Importance of the Converse Chart

Astrologers who fail to use converse charts miss out on many marriage indications. I have found that converse directions were involved almost three times as often as progressed directions at the time of marriage. In fact, the most prevalent aspect of all at marriage was the converse Ascendant/Descendant aspecting a natal or converse love planet. So watch those converse angles carefully!

111

The Progressed Moon as a Marriage Timer

The above aspects give you a possible marriage year, but to zero in for a more exact time, look at the progressed Moon or the outer transits. These set off the progressions.

Since the progressed Moon moves approximately a degree per month, it is usually in aspect to some marriage aspect when the ceremony takes place. Actually, both progressed and converse Moons may be making an exact aspect during the marriage month. Aspects by the converse Moon are more frequent.

Progressed Moon aspects to Mars are the aspects I have seen most frequently as monthly timers. Next come Venus and MC. IC aspects are next. As to the types of progressed Moon aspects, conjunctions are by far most frequent, with trines next, then sextiles. Squares, oppositions, and inconjuncts were at the bottom of the list.

There are also likely to be some interesting aspects from the progressed Moon of one chart to the planets in the partner's chart. We'll look at those in the next chapter, "Love Links Between Charts at the Time of Marriage."

Other Timers

In Chapters Nine and Ten, I'll describe how the Sun/Moon midpoint and some of the Arabic Parts can help foretell marriage years. You'll also see how the Part of Marriage and the Part of Fortune are particularly important in zeroing in on the month of marriage.

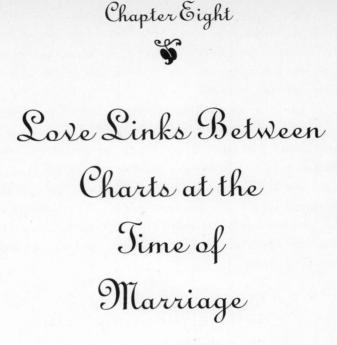

Chapter Eight

Love Links Between
Charts at the
Time of
Marriage

*P*erhaps you've just met someone exciting whom you feel to be Mr. or Ms. Right. Your natal charts match in all the Sun, Moon, Venus, and Mars ways, and each of you have enough current marriage aspects to warrant day-dreaming about rose-covered cottages or condos. But wait a minute! What does astrology say that indicates you two will marry *each other?* Don't jump to such a conclusion before you investigate the "love links" between both updated charts.

The clinchers that can confirm your romantic hopes and dreams will be the links between your progressed and converse directions and those of your potential partner. Sometimes these links are quite eerie and awe-inspiring because they seem so far beyond the laws of probabilities. In fact, you may find it hard to believe when you see their exactness that a marriage was not "made in heaven" or destined from the time you both were born.

I have yet to look at the aspects between two charts at the time of marriage that do not seem to imply that the union was in some way destined or fated. Even those marriages that did not turn out well or did not last have this destined appearance.

I like to believe in free will, and that we create our own reality, but sometimes I wonder about this when I examine the uncanny links between marriage charts. I do recommend, however, that you don't consider these aspects as fatalistic, but use astrology to make informed choices.

114

Other Marriage Links

The love links between planets will not be the only clues. You will also be able to tell whether this is the time, place, and person by looking at planetary transits to both Sun/Moon midpoints—yours and a potential mate's. Pay special attention also to interrelations between each other's planets, angles, and significant Arabic Parts (see Chapter Ten), particularly the Part of Marriage, the Part of Fortune, the Part of Fascination, and the Part of Karma.

The First Step in Looking for Love Links

Look especially to see where your progressed Moon is by sign and degree to observe who might be coming into your life at a particular time. Remember, it takes more than 28 years—or about 360 months—for the progressed Moon to move through all 360 degrees of the zodiac.

So it is rather uncanny when you find you have married a man with his Moon in Aries the very month that your progressed Moon was in Aries conjunct the degree of his natal Moon. Or when you find you have married a woman with her Sun in a certain degree of Virgo within a month of the time that your progressed Moon was at that degree. Or when you have met your current flame the very month that your progressed Moon was conjunct the degree of his or her Sun. (The odds on any of the above "coincidences" are 1 in 360.)

Nineteenth-century astrologer Robert Cross of England, who was known by the name of Raphael, observed such love links at the time of marriage and wrote about it. He stated that if other factors indicate marriage you can tell the month it may happen by looking at the charts of both parties involved and noting the degree of the progressed Moon. When this progressed Moon passes over the degree of the Sun, Moon, or Ascendant of the other person, then marriage may take place. He believed that the conjunction only applied in such cases.

If Cross had used converse directions, he might have noted that the converse Moon as it moves backwards through the 360 degrees of the zodiac often indicates pretty much the same thing. When you look for conjunctions of both progressed Moon and converse Moon to the partner's progressed and converse Moon, as well as to other planets, you will find many cross-links.

Some Interesting Examples of Moon to Moon Links

Often the progressed Moon in one chart will meet at the same degree of the same sign as the converse Moon in the other chart. This means that the two Moons make contact for one month as they pass each other going in opposite directions. James and Marian W. were wed the very month that his progressed Moon was at

3 degrees of Libra and her converse Moon was at 3 degrees of Libra. At the same time, her progressed Moon at 11 degrees of Gemini was conjunct his progressed Mars at 11 degrees of Gemini. In addition, his converse Moon had been conjunct her natal Venus just five months before, a time when they probably met or began to think seriously of a relationship.

Dan and Terri H. were only one month off from a similar progressed-to-converse Moon in passing. Her progressed Moon was going forward at 13 degrees of Capricorn. His converse Moon was going backward and getting ready to conjoin it; it was at 15 degrees of Capricorn the month they were wed. In just one month, the conjunction would take place at 14 degrees of Capricorn. In a way this symbolized that they may have rushed into marriage too soon; the groom was not yet ready for the responsibilities of marriage, but the bride was very impatient to begin a married life.

If a couple have lived together before marriage, you may see that the progressed and converse Moons of the two have already met in passing, the conjunction having taken place a few months earlier.

Most interesting is when both Moons are moving in the same direction together, either both progressed or both converse.

When Ned and Elaine W. eloped, both their progressed Moons were at 24 degrees of Pisces, moving forward together degree by degree. This particular degree in Pisces was especially significant because it trined his Pluto in Cancer and his progressed Mars in Scorpio, forming a grand trine in water signs. At the same time her converse Moon was at 26 degrees of Virgo, conjunct his good luck planet Jupiter. His converse Moon, however, was square her natal Moon, possibly not a good omen; the marriage did ultimately end in divorce.

When Jane Wyman and Ronald Reagan were married, both of their converse Moons were at 25 degrees of Aries. Since this degree was square to his progressed Mars at 25 degrees of Capricorn, and close to a square to his natal Uranus at 26 degrees of

116

Capricorn, there was strife and separation inherent in the marriage from the beginning. Her natal Jupiter was also at 25 degrees of Capricorn, adding to the strong square. They were married for about eight years. It was probably around the time that both converse Moons moved back from 25 degrees of Aries to around 25 degrees of Capricorn that their marriage experienced great difficulties and ultimately broke up.

You'll also see Moon opposite Moon many times by progression or converse direction, as the two Moons make contact from exactly opposite sides of the zodiac. This is not necessarily a separative aspect, since I have seen it in marriages that have lasted a long time.

When Phil and Leonna S. married, their progressed Moons were exactly opposite. Hers was at 8 degrees of Sagittarius, his was at 8 degrees of Gemini. Significant was the fact that they had been together many years before they finally married; the opposition was like a Full Moon, a culmination of hopes and wishes after at least a quarter of a century.

Transiting Jupiter and Uranus were setting off this opposition from around 8 degrees of Sagittarius at the time of the wedding. With their two Moons in the two travel signs, Gemini and Sagittarius, it's not too surprising that they decided to fly to Hawaii for the ceremony.

Vance and Jean M. also had an opposition between her converse Moon at 15 degrees of Scorpio and his natal Moon at 15 degrees of Taurus at the time they met and married within a week. Mars, the planet of passion and haste, was a strong factor in their sudden, rather impulsive wedding plans. His progressed Mars was conjunct her marriage aspect of converse Mars conjunct natal Sun, both on her IC. This marriage, however, has lasted for many years, even though hastily begun.

The Progressed or Converse Moon to the Angles

The progressed or converse Moon of one of the parties conjunct the Ascendant or Descendant of the other is often seen also. Since the Ascendant rules "you" and the Descendant "a partner," when the Moon as a timer contacts the other's axis, the results can be very significant. Such an aspect may bring a strong emotional identification between the two persons, particularly strong in the month that it is exact. For some reason, at the time of the wedding it is often a month or so away from exact in many of the examples I have seen. This can be due to the fact that the Ascendant/Descendant axis is based on the exact time of birth, and the birth times may actually have been a few minutes earlier or later.

Tom B., for instance, had his natal Moon at 8 degrees of Libra; his bride Betty had her converse Descendant at 9 degrees of Libra the month of their wedding; in one month it would have been exact.

There are also the many instances when more than one Moon to Ascendant/Descendant axis takes place, and an averaging-out situation may take place. As an example of this, Frank G. had his progressed Moon at 14 degrees of Leo at his marriage; bride Diane had her converse descendant at 16 degrees of Leo. In two months, the aspect would have been exact. At the same time, Frank's converse Moon at 11 degrees of Aquarius was five months past a conjunction to his bride's converse Descendant at 16 degrees of Aquarius.

The commitment to marriage several months before the wedding may be more important, perhaps, than the actual ceremony. Louise K.'s progressed Moon was at 19 degrees of Gemini, 2 degrees past Brad K.'s natal Descendant of 17 degrees of Gemini at the time of their marriage. Her converse Moon was at 14 degrees of Gemini, 3 degrees past a conjunction.

The progressed Moon changes signs approximately every thirty months. During the time it is traveling through a particular sign, you will often find yourself attracting members of the opposite sex who fit the description of the Moon's sign. The same is true of the converse Moon. If your progressed or converse Moon, for instance, is traveling through Aries, and you have just met an Aries individual, this may be important!

If you have just fallen in love and your progressed Moon will be conjunct the other person's natal Sun by exact degree in a matter of months, you have good cause to hope for a real commitment. At any rate, this is one of the most frequent love links to be found between the charts of bride and groom at the time of marriage.

There are also interesting cases of persons who have known each other for a number of years, but haven't begun thinking of walking down the aisle until such an aspect approached. Howard M. had known Ruth for three or four years. They had talked about marriage, but she didn't agree to set a date until her progressed Moon moved into his Sun sign. At the same time, his converse Moon had moved into her Moon sign.

The progressed or converse Moon to the other's natal Sun is the more frequent aspect because the Moon moves so rapidly. But the reverse can take place. Naylor W. remarried after many years when his converse Sun reached the degree of his bride's natal Moon. At the same time, her progressed Moon was going through his Sun sign.

Other Love Links

Although not as frequently as the Moon/Moon, Moon/Ascendant/Descendant, or Moon/Sun, you'll also find interrelations between charts of other combinations of the four love planets — Sun, Moon, Venus, and Mars.

One person's progressed Venus conjunct the other's natal Sun, for example, can be a potent love factor, or Venus conjunct the other person's Mars, or any of these factors in aspects to an angle in the other's chart. There will generally be at least three or more such love links at the time of marriage.

What seems to happen is that a person with marriage aspects at certain degrees of the zodiac attracts a mate who has marriage aspects at similar degrees. The charts of Ned and Elaine W. provide some excellent examples of this. In the previous section on Moon-to-Moon links, you saw how their progressed Moons were moving forward at the same degree of the zodiac. There were many other links.

One of Elaine's most important marriage aspects was of progressed Mars to an angle, her converse IC. This is an aspect I have discovered in many women's marriage-year charts. Mars was at 2 degrees of Leo, her IC at 3 degrees of Leo. His converse Sun was in orb at 4 degrees of Leo. His converse Moon was sextile at 2 degrees of Libra.

Another of Elaine's marriage aspects was a Sun/Descendant combination. Her converse Sun was at 19 degrees of Pisces; her converse Descendant was trine at 20 degrees of Scorpio. His progressed Venus just happened to be at 20 degrees of Scorpio, right on her Descendant.

Elaine's converse Venus, the planet of love, was that year conjunct her natal Ascendant ruler, Mercury. This pair just happened to be exactly opposite his Jupiter, the planet of good fortune.

In addition, Elaine's progressed Jupiter, the ruler of her seventh house of marriage, had retrograded to 20 degrees of Libra, trining her natal Ascendant at 20 degrees of Gemini and sextile her natal Descendant at 20 degrees of Sagittarius, a superb marriage aspect. His converse Ascendant that year at 20 degrees of Aquarius and his converse Descendant at 20 degrees of Leo added a few sextiles and trines to this marriage aspect.

Chapter Nine

The Sun / Moon
Midpoint as a
Marriage Indicator
and Timer

So you think you have a perfect chart with someone. Or maybe it's almost a perfect match, but you're hoping it will work out anyway. If you're really serious about the relationship—or think you could be, you'd better check out the Sun/Moon midpoint ties before you go any further.

I've found that no matter how compatible two horoscopes may seem to be, two people seldom marry or sustain a serious relationship unless one of the following indications is seen between the two charts.

- The Sun/Moon midpoint of one partner is in hard aspect to the Sun or Moon of the other. (A hard aspect includes the conjunction, square, opposition, semisquare, or sesquisquare.)
- The composite Sun/Moon midpoint is in hard aspect to the Sun or Moon of one or both of the partners. (The composite Sun/Moon midpoint will be explained later in this chapter.)

What's a Sun/Moon Midpoint?

For those who may not know what the Sun/Moon midpoint is, it's the marriage-sensitive point halfway between the degree of your Sun (ruling the masculine principle) and the degree of your Moon (ruling the female principle). Anyone with a planet there on your Sun/Moon midpoint is going to have an effect on your romantic life or your marriage, but if your potential mate has his or her Sun or Moon on that degree, that's an indicator you're not just imagining the attraction. This could be it!

As an example, let's say your Sun is at 5 degrees of Aries and your Moon is at 25 degrees of Aries. That's an easy one to figure. There would be 20 degrees between your Sun and your Moon. Divide that in half to find the midway point. Half of the distance is 10 degrees. Add 10 degrees to the earlier planet, the Sun at 5 degrees of Aries. Your Sun/Moon midpoint turns out to be 15 degrees of Aries. If you run into someone with *their* Sun or Moon at 15 degrees of Aries, you have a valid Sun/Moon midpoint tie. (Of course, with all this Aries influence between the two of you, you may have a pretty wild and action-packed relationship as well!)

A Long-Term Marriage

A great example of this principle shows up in the charts of those wonders of the Hollywood-marriage-world, Paul Newman and Joanne Woodward. Their lengthy, happy marriage has defied tinsel-town customs and conventions. Her Sun is at 8 degrees of

122

Pisces; her Moon is in the preceding sign at around 25 degrees of Aquarius. From 25 degrees of Aquarius to 8 degrees of Pisces is about 13 degrees. Half of that is 6-1/2. Add that to the earlier degree: 25 degrees of Aquarius plus 6-1/2 equals 1-1/2 degrees of Pisces. That's her Sun/Moon midpoint. Newman's Moon is almost exactly at 1-1/2 degrees of Pisces. Voila!

A Long-Term Relationship

I have already pointed out the incredibly favorable aspects between newspaper mogul William Randolph Hearst and his long-time mistress, actress Marion Davies. Their luxurious tenure at Hearst Castle in San Simeon, California, is legendary. Let's look at his Sun/Moon midpoint. With Sun at 8 degrees of Taurus and Moon at 17 degrees of Virgo, his Sun/Moon midpoint would fall half-way between at around 12-1/2 degrees of Cancer. (If you are not familiar with finding midpoints, I'll show you how to figure this later.) Her Sun is at 13 degrees of Capricorn. No, this is not a conjunction, but an opposition. Cancer and Capricorn are opposite signs.

Does that work? You bet. In the world of midpoint astrology, squares and oppositions are considered to be as valid as conjunctions in triggering sensitive midpoints. In working with midpoints, just forget about oppositions being differences or pulling apart, and squares being conflicts.

Getting Back to You

So, let's say you have your Sun/Moon midpoint at 15 degrees of Aries. The degree opposite, which would be 15 degrees of Libra, is equally sensitive. So are the degrees square, 15 degrees of Cancer and 15 degrees of Capricorn. If the other party's Sun or Moon are on or near these degrees, you also have a valid indication that there's something serious going on. So you have four locations that reflect the Sun/Moon midpoint energies—15 degrees of Aries, 15

Aries = 0° to 29°

Taurus = 30 to 59°

Gemini = 60° to 89°

Cancer = 90° to 119°

Leo = 120° to 149°

Virgo = 150° to 179°

Libra = 180° to 209°

Scorpio = 210° to 239°

Sagittarius = 240° to 269°

Capricorn = 270° to 299°

Aquarius = 300° to 329°

Pisces = 330° to 359°

360 Degree Conversion Table

degrees of Cancer, 15 degrees of Libra, and 15 degrees of Capricorn. You might notice that these are the four Cardinal signs.

If you haven't learned the classification of signs into Cardinal, Fixed, and Mutable, here it is:

Cardinal (leadership): Aries, Cancer, Libra, and Capricorn.

Fixed (stability): Taurus, Leo, Scorpio, and Aquarius.

Mutable (flexibility): Gemini, Virgo, Sagittarius, and Pisces.

To figure your Sun/Moon midpoint, it's easiest if you change the degrees of the zodiac into numbers from zero to 359. The first thirty degrees represent Aries. The next thirty degrees are those of Taurus, and so on. A conversion table is shown above.

An Example of Figuring the Midpoint

Let's take the charts of Prince Charles and Princess Diana of Britain to show how to use the conversion table on the preceding page. In their case it is her Sun/Moon midpoint that is in aspect to his Sun. Her Sun is at 9 degrees of Cancer; her Moon at 25 degrees of Aquarius. Looking at the table, we see that the sign Cancer begins at 90. That would equate with 0 degrees of Cancer. Then add 9 degrees for her Sun. That gives 99. Her Moon at 25 degrees of Aquarius equates to 300 + 25 or 325. Next, add together the degrees of Sun and Moon:

$$99° + 325° = 424°$$

125

Then divide the above figure in half: half of 424 is 212. That represents the midpoint. Referring to the table, you'll see that 212 falls into the sign Scorpio. It is just 2 degrees beyond zero degrees of Scorpio. Thus, it would be 2 degrees of Scorpio.

Prince Charles' Moon is at zero degrees of Taurus, fairly close to an opposition to this point. Thus his Moon is in opposition to her Sun/Moon midpoint.

Minor Aspects That Will Also Work

We call squares and oppositions "hard aspects." These are the aspects that work best with midpoints. There are also two types of "minor aspects" that are also considered hard aspects because they are based on the principle of the square.

They are the semisquare (45 degrees—which is half a square) and the sesquisquare (135 degrees—which is a square and a half). In looking for Sun/Moon midpoint ties, you can also use these. They are equally valid.

To discover if a potential mate has a minor aspect Sun/Moon midpoint tie with you, first find your Sun/Moon midpoint. Let's say it turns out to be 15 degrees of Aries, as in the example above. You know that a mate's Sun or Moon should be at 15 degrees of the Cardinal signs, as we explained above. To find if that mate's Sun or Moon is in minor aspect to your midpoint, do this: Add 45 degrees to your Sun/Moon midpoint. (Use the conversion table on page 124 if you need to.)

15° Aries + 45° = 0° Gemini

Gemini is a mutable sign: You can easily find all the semisquares and sesquisquares to your midpoint by looking at all four of the mutable signs: zero degrees of Gemini, zero degrees of Virgo, zero degrees of Sagittarius, and zero degrees of Pisces are the degrees where a mate's Sun or Moon might also be.

126

Minor Aspects Don't Mean the Passion Isn't Major

An example of a couple who related on minor aspects involves one of the greatest love stories of all time, that of poets Robert Browning and Elizabeth Barrett Browning. As I mentioned in Chapter One, theirs was one of the soul-mate unions that poets write about. Her Sun/Moon midpoint was 28 degrees of Sagittarius. His Sun was 17 degrees of Taurus. Her midpoint was within sesquisquare orb to his Sun. But there was also a minor aspect from her Moon to their composite Sun/Moon midpoint—another very important point.

The Composite Sun/Moon Midpoint

The composite Sun/Moon midpoint is a sensitive point in the relationship. It is half-way between the two partners' Sun/Moon midpoints. To find a composite Sun/Moon midpoint, just add together both midpoints, yours and his or hers, and divide by two. This is also a remarkably sensitive point between the two charts. You may well find either your Sun or Moon, or the mate's Sun or Moon on this degree, or in hard aspect to it.

The Duke and Duchess of Windsor, for example, related in marriage through this aspect. Their composite Sun/Moon midpoint was square her Sun.

Your Progressed or Converse Sun

There may also be strong Sun/Moon midpoint ties to your partner's progressed or converse Sun at the time you meet or marry. You probably learned your progressed and converse Sun positions in studying Chapter Seven. The progressed Sun moves forward through the zodiac at approximately one degree per year of age. If your natal Sun is at 5 degrees of Aries, for instance, by age 20 it will be around 25 degrees of Aries. At that age, you might meet and marry an individual with a Sun/Moon midpoint at 25 degrees of Aries or in hard aspect to that degree.

I have yet to find a marriage or strong relationship where there was not some sort of tie-up between a Sun/Moon midpoint and the Sun or Moon of one of the parties.

Here are some other examples: John F. Kennedy's Sun/Moon midpoint at 27 degrees of Cancer was square Jackie's Moon at 25 degrees of Aries. Her Sun/Moon midpoint at 15 degrees of Gemini was seven degrees from a conjunction to his Sun. Here the aspect worked both ways.

With poets Robert and Elizabeth Barrett Browning, the natal aspects were less strong. Most of the strength of their passionate union came through progressed planets. Natally, there was only a sesquiquadrate (135 degrees) from their composite Sun/Moon midpoint to her Moon. But when they met, the progressed Sun/Moon midpoint ties were overpoweringly strong.

Similarly, Clark Gable and Carole Lombard had natally only a semisquare from their composite Sun/Moon midpoint to her Sun. The stronger aspects came by progression at the time they married.

The Sun/Moon Midpoint as a Marriage Timer

The Sun/Moon midpoint when contacted by important transits can also be a vital marriage timer. These midpoints become activated when one of the outer planets—Pluto, Neptune, Uranus, Saturn, or Jupiter—passes over them by transit. A quick way to discover if a person you have just met is ready for a serious relationship such as marriage is to check the midpoint between their Sun and Moon.

Then note if Uranus or one of the other outer planets is soon to pass over the degree of that midpoint. Of course, you would want to do the same for yourself to see if marriage could be coming up for you in the near future.

Most people at the time of marriage have from one to four hard aspects from the transiting outer planets to their own Sun/Moon midpoint or to the couples' composite Sun/Moon midpoint. Allow a two or three degree orb of the transiting planet to the point. Hard aspects, remember, include the conjunction, the square (90 degrees), the opposition (180 degrees), the semisquare (45 degrees), and the sesquisquare (135 degrees).

It's a good idea to keep a record of the degrees in hard aspect to your Sun/Moon midpoint so that you'll know when marriage possibilities may be approaching. The transits of the outer planets which are conjunct, square, or in opposition to your Sun/Moon midpoint will be easy to spot from just a glance in an ephemeris of the planets' current places, but the semisquares and sesquisquares may not be as easy to determine without a little math.

Many people, however, won't have to worry about the minor aspects since the marriage transits will be so obvious. Mary K.'s Sun/Moon midpoint, for instance, was 27 degrees of Sagittarius. Her husband's was 24 degrees of Scorpio. Their composite Sun/Moon was at 10 degrees of Sagittarius.

Here's how the transits of the outer planets looked on their wedding day. It was just after the start of World War II, and he was about to be shipped overseas.

Jupiter at 12 degrees of Sagittarius — conjunct the composite midpoint.

Uranus at 26 degrees of Taurus — opposite his Sun/Moon at 24 degrees of Scorpio.

Saturn at 21 degrees of Taurus — opposite his Sun/Moon at 24 degrees of Scorpio.

Neptune at 29 degrees of Virgo — square her Sun/Moon at 27 degrees of Sagittarius.

Ruth and Howard M.'s pattern was not as easy to spot visually because semisquares were involved. Here's how the outer planet transits looked when they wed:

Neptune at 12 degrees of Libra — semisquare her Sun/Moon at 17 degrees of Leo.

Uranus at 1 degree of Cancer — semisquare her Sun/Moon at 17 degrees of Leo.

Pluto at 15 degrees of Leo — conjunct her Sun/Moon at 17 degrees of Leo.

Jupiter at zero degrees of Aquarius — square his Sun/Moon at 1 degree of Taurus.

One couple had only one outer planet in such aspect. Sara and Bill C. had only Uranus conjunct her Sun/Moon at their wedding. The transiting Sun, which apparently acted as a timer for the wedding day, was conjunct the composite Sun/Moon but there was little else. In most cases, however, you'll find more aspects than just a single outer-planet transit. Of course, if a couple have been living together for some time, these transits may have taken place at an earlier date when they really began to see themselves as a couple.

How Progressed Planets Can Affect Sun/Moon Midpoints

One of the most romantic marriages in history was that of poets Robert Browning and Elizabeth Barrett Browning. Her progressed Sun had moved from sensitive Pisces to fiery Aries when they met and ran away together. She was a forty-year-old recluse, practically a prisoner in her father's Victorian home. He was a thirty-four-year-old young man who admired her poetry.

There was a great deal of planetary energy to promote their subsequent romance and marriage. Her progressed Sun in Aries just happened to have moved to the degree of his Sun/Moon midpoint—24 degrees of Aries—when he began to court her. Both transiting Jupiter and Pluto were at 24 degrees of Aries during that time. During the same period, Neptune in transit was around 26 degrees of Aquarius, the degree of their composite Sun/Moon midpoint.

When they married the following year, Pluto was still conjoining his Sun/Moon midpoint at 24 degrees of Aries, while both Saturn and Neptune were conjunct the composite Sun/Moon. In addition, on their wedding day, Venus was opposite the composite Sun/Moon midpoint.

How Converse Planets Can Affect Sun/Moon Midpoints

A more unusual case, because of the startling coincidences (if such they were), involved two more contemporary lovers. Roy and Rita were both Virgos; both had Moons in Cancer. His Sun/Moon midpoint was 24 degrees, 09 minutes of Leo. Her Sun/Moon midpoint was 17 degrees, 39 minutes of Leo. The composite Sun/Moon midpoint was 20 degrees, 54 minutes of Leo. The evening they met at a party transiting Uranus was within a degree of conjoining this composite Sun/Moon midpoint.

Both had the planet Neptune in Leo, and the midpoint of their two Neptunes was 24 degrees, 40 minutes of Leo, right on his Sun/Moon midpoint. In addition, his North Node was at 20 degrees, 57 minutes of Leo, closely conjunct the composite Sun/Moon midpoint. (Neptune at the Sun/Moon midpoint was not an entirely good aspect. Although there was much sharing of ideals and spiritual interests, the closeness of Neptune, especially to *his* Sun/Moon midpoint, finally led to a dissolution of the marriage.)

A strong and unusual tie, however, was the fact that their converse Suns were conjunct and would always be because he was three years older and had been born three days later in the month than she. Both of their Virgo Suns had moved backwards by converse direction into Leo, and at the time they met were at 24 degrees of Leo—the degree of his Sun/Moon midpoint.

By the time they married, both converse Suns had moved back to 22 degrees of Leo. On the day they wed, transiting Mars and Uranus were at 22 degrees of Leo, and both were right on Rita's converse IC. As a timer, the transiting Sun was sextile at 22 degrees of Gemini.

The degrees between 18 and 24 of Leo continued to be important factors in events in their marriage. They bought a house and moved in on a day when Moon and Mars were at 23 degrees of Leo. Some years later, marriage ties began eroding when Neptune squared their composite Sun/Moon midpoint from Scorpio. On the day she left him, there was a Full Moon squaring her Sun/Moon midpoint. Neptune, which often symbolizes idealism, can also indicate a more platonic than physical type of relationship, and this was one of the main reasons for the breakup. Only years later did she learn that while they were married he had been deceiving her (Neptune) in an involvement with someone else.

Chapter Ten

Arabic Parts
and
Karmic Ties

So the person you have in mind meets all the criteria—or most of it—for an eligible match, but there's all the difference in the world between an eligible match and that heaven-sent special person who seems like a soul mate to you.

You can usually distinguish the latter type by your feelings, but if you want to be really sure, you can use the techniques in this chapter to verify what your heart tells you. These are the techniques that indicate whether it's a fated union with links that defy the laws of averages.

These links include Arabic Parts, nodal connections, and other indications of karmic love.

Comparing Charts With the Arabic Parts

For comparing charts of lovers, I use four Arabic Parts: The Part of Fortune, the Part of Marriage, the Part of Fascination, and the Part of Karma. There are numerous other Arabic Parts, most of very ancient origin. An Arabian astrologer, Al-Biruni, listed 158 of them in a book he wrote in A.D. 1029. He had collected them from all over the world, from civilizations older than his. Since the Arabs used them extensively, the name "Arabic Parts" has become identified with them.

Since then, modern astrologers have added others that they have found to be effective. In my experience, the four mentioned above are the most effective in discovering meaningful links between potential mates.

How to Find Your Arabic Parts

If you are not familiar with the concept of Arabic Parts, you should know that they are based on distances between various points and planets in a chart. You find them through formulas based on the Ascendant degree (usually) plus another planet or point minus a third planet or point. The formula is A+B-C.

Most astrology computer programs list the Part of Fortune automatically when they print out a chart. The symbol for it is a circle with an X in the middle. If your computer program does not list this or the other Arabic Parts listed above, you can figure them rather easily through use of the conversion table on page 124 in Chapter Nine. Here's an example of how to figure the most commonly used of these points, the Part of Fortune.

The formula for this is Ascendant plus Moon minus Sun. Using the chart of Britain's Princess Diana, here is how to find her Part of Fortune:

As you can see on page 75 in Chapter Five, her Ascendant is 18 degrees of Sagittarius; her Moon is 25 degrees of Aquarius; and her Sun is 9 degrees of Cancer.

Ascendant at 18° Sagittarius = 258 degrees

plus Moon at 25° Aquarius = 325 degrees

Sub Total= 583 degrees

minus Sun at 9° Cancer = 99 degrees

Total = 484 degrees

Since we have arrived at a total that is more than 360 degrees, we must subtract 360 degrees from our total:

Total = 484 degrees

minus 360° = 360 degrees

Total = 124 degrees = 4° Leo

That's her Part of Fortune.

The Part of Fortune Between Charts

In her own chart, Princess Diana's Part of Fortune falls in her eighth house of other people's money. Thus her good fortune comes through inheritance or the assets of a partner. In the Prince's chart, her Part of Fortune is conjunct his Ascendant, which is around 5 degrees of Leo. With the four Arabic Parts I use in comparing charts, I frequently see such conjunctions to an important place in the partner's chart.

Frank Sinatra's Part of Fortune provides some interesting examples. It is located in his own chart at 14 degrees of Capricorn conjunct his Venus, a love planet. Since both are in his third house of self-expression and communication, you can see why he has been so fortunate in expressing himself through love songs. Many romances have blossomed to the background of his ballads. Marilyn Monroe used to listen to his records while putting herself into the proper mood for photography sessions. Since his Part of Fortune fell on the cusp of her sixth house of work, this is not too surprising.

I don't have the charts of all of the women who have played roles in Sinatra's life, but in those charts I do have, his Part of Fortune is significantly placed. Sinatra was married briefly to actress Ava Gardner, but the union didn't last. His Part of Fortune was conjunct her Mercury of communication in her fifth house of romance. However, it opposed her Pluto. This could have made for an intense relationship with many power plays.

Sinatra was also married for a matter of months to actress Mia Farrow. His Part of Fortune fell on her Moon, which rules emotion, moods, and one's feminine nature.

136

The Arabic Part of Marriage

This is probably the most important point in your chart or in a partner's as far as marriage is concerned. The formula for it is Ascendant plus Descendant minus Venus.

In your own chart, the Part of Marriage often indicates the type of marriage you will have by the aspects it makes to other planets. One man had this part conjunct his Neptune (secrecy) in his fourth house of family. He had been married secretly; he felt he could not tell his parents about it. The Part of Marriage is also frequently a timer that indicates when marriage will take place.

Your Part of Marriage will most often be conjunct your mate's Sun, Moon, Ascendant, Descendant, Midheaven, or IC (fourth house cusp). Frequently, I have found the Part of Marriage to conjoin a partner's Saturn, as well as other planets. You'll also find some interesting conjunctions of this part with the mate's Parts of Fortune, Fascination, or Karma.

None of the above connections, however, between Part of Marriage and another's chart placements guarantee a lasting union. Some of the marriages with these links have ended in divorce, while others have been life-long alliances.

Probably a Part of Marriage connection with another chart triggers a strong impulse to marry, even if the marriage does not make much sense to outside observers. One partner might be much older than the other, for instance, or not the type you'd expect the person to select as a mate. The impulse to marry seems to be especially strong when both Parts of Marriage are linked to a planet or point in another's chart.

When Frank Sinatra married Mia Farrow, for example, many people may have been puzzled. This was an alliance where there was a great difference in age and experience, and the stormy marriage didn't last long. Why did he marry Mia rather than the many other women he had dated over the years?

They did have some good aspects between their two charts. His Sun in Sagittarius was sextile her Sun in Aquarius. Her Moon in Capricorn was almost exactly conjunct his Venus, indicating a social/love tie. They had some weak Mars/Venus ties for sexual attraction; his Mars was at 27 degrees of Leo, and her Venus was also in a fire sign at 7 degrees of Aries, but there was no trine aspect. Her Mars was at 26 degrees of Capricorn and his Venus at 11 degrees of Capricorn; they were in the same sign but not in orb by degree. His Sun/Moon midpoint was conjunct her Mars, but not her Sun or Moon, possibly an indication of a great deal of Martian strife. His midpoint was, however, in minor hard aspect to her Moon. Her own Sun/Moon midpoint, at 1 degree of Aquarius, was only in hard aspect to his Neptune at 2 degrees of Leo. This could have led to some illusions or confusion.

Some of the above spelled a possible marriage, at least an attraction, but their Parts of Marriage showed me why they tied the knot, if only temporarily. The strong impulse to a union came from his Part of Marriage at 18 degrees of Aquarius, conjunct her Sun, and her Part of Marriage at 13 degrees of Sagittarius, close to *his* Sun.

There were also additional Arabic Part ties as we shall see in the sections on the Part of Fascination and the Part of Karma.

137

Other Two-Way Marriage Ties

It does seem to make the impulse to marry stronger when the conjunction to the Part of Marriage is seen in both charts. A long-lasting marriage, that of Paul Newman and Joanne Woodward, has this strong link. His Part of Marriage at 11 degrees of Cancer is conjunct her Descendant. Her Part of Marriage at 10 degrees of Taurus is conjunct his Descendant. Since the Descendant is the point in the chart associated with marriage, this is an incredibly strong two-way aspect. They are fortunate for each other in partnership.

A long-lasting marriage, but one that finally ended in her mental illness and a divorce, was that of the screen's "Scarlet O'Hara," Vivien Leigh, and British actor Lawrence Olivier. His Part of Marriage at 2 degrees of Aquarius was conjunct Leigh's Moon, Uranus, and Midheaven. Her Part of Marriage at 23 degrees of Taurus was in orb of Olivier's Sun at 29 degrees of Taurus.

A Long-Term Relationship

Unlike her short union with Frank Sinatra, Mia Farrow had a long-lasting relationship with Woody Allen. (Although it now seems to be at an end.) Like Frank Sinatra, Allen is a Sagittarian. Mia's Part of Marriage is also close to his Sun. This is also a two-way link. Woody's Part of Marriage is exactly on her Moon in Capricorn. There is also a close Sun/Moon midpoint link here, with his midpoint conjunct her Moon. One of the closest ties they have is her Sun in Aquarius conjunct his Moon in Aquarius.

Frequency of the Types of Aspects

In my research, conjunctions of the Part of Marriage to the angles of the chart—Ascendant, Descendant, Midheaven, or Nadir (IC)—were most often seen. Next in frequency were aspects to the other's Sun. However, aspects to the other's Saturn were surprisingly strong.

One other type of conjunction that I found in long-lasting and happy unions was Part of Marriage conjunct the mate's fifth house cusp. Since the fifth house rules creativity and children, one or the other—or both of these—can be rather important in such marriages.

The Arabic Part of Fascination

Another important link when marriage takes place is between one partner's Part of Fascination and the other's Sun, Moon, or other important planet or point. In one marriage I know of, the wife's Part of Fascination is conjunct the husband's Moon, and his part of Fascination is conjunct her Sun. You don't always find such an ideal set-up, however. If you do, you've probably found a soulmate.

Astrologer Marc Edmond Jones was first to call this formula the Part of Fascination. To locate it, you add your Ascendant to Venus and subtract Uranus. As an example, let's find Mia Farrow's Part of Fascination. Her Ascendant is 10 degrees of Taurus; her Venus is 7 degrees of Aries, and her Uranus is 9 degrees of Gemini. (Use the conversion table on page 124.)

Ascendant at 10° Taurus =   40
plus Venus at 7° Aries =   7
Subtotal =   47
minus Uranus at 9° Gemini =   69

In order to subtract a larger number from a smaller, you will have to add 360 degrees to the smaller number as follows:

Subtotal =   47
plus 360° = 360
Subtotal = 407
minus Uranus at 9° Gemini =   69
Total = 338 = 8° Pisces

Since Sinatra's Moon is at 5 degrees of Pisces, Farrow's Part of Fascination formed a conjunction to his Moon. His Part of Fascination, at 27 degrees of Virgo was conjunct Farrow's Jupiter (and her Part of Karma). These were some pretty potent ties. There may have been something they had to finish up from a past life because of the involvement of the Part of Karma.

With Woody Allen, Farrow's Part of Fascination is conjunct his Saturn. Since Saturn often brings long-lasting ties, this may account for the longer length of this relationship. Saturn also represents a greater-than-usual age difference, as well as some lesson to be learned. In addition, his Part of Fascination is conjunct her Sun. At any rate, you can see from these examples the importance of Part of Fascination links and the planet they connect with in a partner's chart. Only conjunctions seem to work. Use an orb of about 6 degrees.

The Part of Karma and Other Karmic Indications

If you feel you've known your partner somewhere, but can't remember "where or when," you'll probably want to check out the Part of Karma, plus several other points in the chart that seem to indicate past-life involvement. Not every relationship is a karmic tie. Some relationships seem to be karmic, but not as strongly so as others.

The Part of Karma is not found in significant conjunction to a mate's planets or points as frequently as the Arabic Parts mentioned above. When you do find it in significant relationship to the other chart, you should also check out the other karmic connections which will be discussed later in this chapter. The more you find, the more probability there is of a past-life tie.

The formula for the Part of Karma is Ascendant plus Saturn minus the Sun. The most frequent placements I have found which seem strongly karmic involve the woman's Part of Karma conjunct the husband's or lover's sun.

140

This is frequently a theme in famous love stories. Elizabeth Barrett Browning's Part of Karma related in this way to Robert Browning's Sun. So did Jacqueline Kennedy Onassis' Part of Karma to the Sun of John F. Kennedy. The Duke and Duchess of Windsor related in this way as well. Also with this pattern were the charts of Britain's Restoration monarch, Charles II, and longtime mistress Nell Gwyn, the little cockney girl who stole his heart.

Important, too, are connections between one partner's Part of Karma and a mate's planet. Joanne Woodward's Part of Karma is conjunct Paul Newman's Saturn; Liz Taylor's conjunct Mike Todd's Moon and Richard Burton's Neptune; Prince Charles' to Princess Diana's Venus. The symbolism of the planet involved will tell you something about what they may have been to each other in the past.

141

The third most often seen connection is that of the Part of Karma of one to a point in the other's chart. William Randolph Hearst's Part of Karma was conjunct Marion Davies' Midheaven, while her Part of Karma was conjunct his Part of Marriage. These two-way ties make for an especially fated type of relationship. You'll often see the Part of Karma of one conjunct an angle of the other's chart, or to other points associated with a fated relationship, such as the Vertex or the South Node.

One very special relationship is when both Parts of Karma are close to the same degree of the zodiac. I've seen this in the charts of persons who have many other indications of a karmic tie in their charts as well.

Nodal Connections

The location of the South Node of the Moon in your chart has much to tell about your karmic past. The sign and the house this point occupies in your chart can tell the story. The South Node also indicates where you must sacrifice, or give. The Duke of Windsor, for instance, had his South Node at 5 degrees of Libra (the sign of marriage) in his eighth house of joint finances. He gave up or sacrificed a kingdom in exchange for marriage to the woman he loved.

The fact that they shared this karma is suggested by the Duchess of Windsor's eighth house cusp at 5 degrees of Libra conjunct his South Node. This suggests there was a mutual karmic debt, having to do with marriage and possessions, owed each other from the karmic past.

Her own South Node, at 26 degrees of Leo, is in her seventh house of partners. With the South Node in the sign of royalty, she married a king, but was not permitted to become a queen. Looking at this in a karmic way, she may have been born of a royal family in a past life; who knows what royal dramas may have occurred in their past lives together.

There are many good books that discuss the lunar Nodes. My purpose here is to show only the South Node's importance as a factor in karmic ties. If you wish to know more about the Nodes in general, I recommend Bernice Prill Grebner's book, *Lunar Nodes: New Concepts,* published by the American Federation of Astrologers in Tempe, Arizona.

One of the most frequent ties I have seen between the charts of marriage partners is one South Node conjunct the other's Moon. This is especially important because the Moon also has much to do with the karmic past.

You'll also often see the South Node of one person conjunct an Arabic Part or house cusp in the mate's chart. The Arabic Parts of Karma and Fortune are the two I have noted most often. Of house cusps, a conjunction of one person's South Node to the other's IC (or fourth house cusp) is most frequent. This is especially interesting because the IC is also a point believed to indicate past life connections; the fourth house has connotations of one's life foundations.

The Vertex as an Indication of Fated Attractions

If you have a computer print-out of your natal chart, you may note a point in one of the houses on the right-hand side of the chart marked VX, standing for Vertex. This is a third angle of the chart.

It is important because conjunctions of one person's planets to this point in your chart is also frequently an indication of a fatedness about the union. Clark Gable's Vertex, for instance, was conjunct wife Carole Lombard's Part of Karma and Venus.

In my research of marriage charts, Neptune of one person conjunct the Vertex of the other was the most frequent planetary tie. Sun, Moon, and Venus were close behind. Since Neptune ties between charts can indicate innate psychic understanding of each other, they are often karmic in nature. Neptune to Moon aspects between charts, for instance, will often accompany many other indications of past life involvement.

Arabic Parts and house cusps most often conjunct a partner's Vertex are the Part of Fortune, Part of Karma, and the IC.

Another Test for Karmic Ties

Between your chart and a partner's chart, consider the interaction of the Moon, the IC, the Moon's ruler and the IC ruler. These show karmic connections, particularly if there is a close conjunction of two of the above. It becomes especially strong if evident in relation to both persons' IC and Moon. Astrologer Raymond Merriman, who has lectured on evolutionary astrology for many years, is the one who has researched this information and proposes this theory. As mentioned in the above section, both Moon and IC rule the past.

Here are possible ways of relating Moon and IC:

1. One Moon is conjunct the other IC.
2. One Moon is conjunct the other IC ruler.
3. The ruler of one Moon is conjunct the other IC ruler.
4. The ruler of one Moon is conjunct the other IC.

To determine whether you relate karmically to another individual according to this theory, list these placements in your chart and in a partner's chart:

	Your Chart	Partner's Chart
Moon		
Moon Ruler		
IC		
IC Ruler		

To show you how this is done, the placements of the Duke and Duchess of Windsor are shown below.

	His Chart	**Her Chart**
Moon	4 Pisces	21 Libra
Moon Ruler	Neptune at 14 Gemini	Venus at 23 Gemini
IC	2 Gemini	5 Gemini
IC Ruler	Mercury at 27 Cancer	Mercury at 16 Gemini

Note the conjunction between his Moon ruler (Neptune) and her IC ruler (Mercury). Note also that IC is conjunct IC.

One of the most interesting examples I have seen of the above evolutionary ties is in the charts of a couple who already have strong karmic ties shown by other factors in their charts, such as Parts of Karma conjunct, Moon/Neptune interactions, and strong Nodal connections. Her Moon is conjunct his IC, and his Moon ruler is conjunct her IC. These two share many interests in common, probably from past life involvement.

To refresh your memory as to sign rulers, here they are:

Aries is ruled by Mars

Taurus is ruled by Venus

Gemini is ruled by Mercury

Cancer is ruled by Moon

Leo is ruled by the Sun

Virgo is ruled by Mercury

Libra is ruled by Venus

Scorpio is ruled by Pluto

Sagittarius is ruled by Jupiter

Capricorn is ruled by Saturn

Aquarius is ruled by Uranus

Pisces is ruled by Neptune

A Karmic Summary

The main planets and points that seem to indicate karmic connections are the following: Moon, Neptune, Part of Karma, South Node, Vertex, and the IC. Check all of these in both charts for conjunctions to each other in order to find possible past life ties.

Love Links Between Karmic Ties at the Time of Marriage

The Part of Marriage as a Timer

Your Part of Marriage will usually make some aspect to your partner's Sun, Moon, Ascendant, Descendant, MC, IC, or even to Saturn or one of the other key Arabic Parts.

As was pointed out in the chapter on progressions, a rough estimate of a marriage year can be made by adding your age to the degree of the natal Part of Marriage. The year that it makes an important aspect to a love planet or seventh house ruler can be a marriage year, but this is just a rough preliminary way of estimating a marriage year, and does not work as well in some charts as others.

The Part of Marriage works even better as a marriage timer if you figure it anew from your current progressed and converse charts. Just use your progressed and converse Ascendants, Descendants, and places of Venus instead of the natal degrees. An example using the chart of Ned W. follows.

His natal Part of Marriage was exactly conjunct Elaine's natal Sun. During the year of his marriage to her, his progressed Part of Marriage became 10 degrees of Aquarius, trine his natal Venus (a love planet and ruler of his seventh house) at 10 degrees of Libra. His converse Part of Marriage became 10 degrees of Gemini, also trine his Venus. A grand trine was formed in his chart by progressed and converse Parts of Marriage.

His bride's natal Part of Marriage was at 8 degrees of Aquarius, close to his progressed Part of Marriage and one degree from his progressed Saturn the year they wed. Her progressed Part of Marriage became 20 degrees of Aquarius, trine her natal Ascendant, and sextile her natal Descendant. Her converse Part of Marriage was at 9 degrees of Capricorn, close to her progressed Descendant.

Ruth M. had progressed Part of Marriage at 21 degrees of Sagittarius, conjunct her converse Descendant, at her first marriage. Her converse Part of Marriage, at 21 degrees of Virgo, was conjunct converse Mars and close to converse Venus. Note the exact square between the two Parts of Marriage.

146

At her second marriage, Ruth had progressed Part of Marriage conjunct her new husband's Ascendant and square her own natal Mars. Her converse Part of Marriage was close to trine the progressed Part of Marriage.

The Part of Fortune as a Marriage Timer

This Arabic Part is also one of the most significant marriage timers as it moves forward or backward at the rate of about a degree per month. Since this Arabic Part is composed of masculine Sun, feminine Moon and the axis of partnership, Ascendant and Descendant, it can be seen to be very symbolic of marriage itself. In fact, to the ancients this same formula was used for the Time of Marriage.

Figure it anew in each progressed or converse chart from the new degrees for Ascendant, Moon, and Sun. Since the progressed and converse Moons move respectively forward and backward at the rate of about one degree a month, they can be timers for the exact month of marriage.

Your progressed or converse Part of Fortune during the month when marriage takes place will make a significant aspect, usually a conjunction to a planet or angle in your chart that has to do with love, marriage, or partnership. There will frequently be an aspect like this to your own chart, and also to your partner's chart. Here are the aspects I have seen most often:

Part of Fortune to Ascendant or Descendant

Look particularly for conjunctions to the Ascendant and/or Descendant of all three charts—natal, progressed, and converse. This is where I have most frequently found the Part of Fortune to be during the month of marriage.

For instance, Bob K., the month he married, had his progressed Part of Fortune at 19 degrees of Sagittarius, two degrees from his natal Ascendant and exactly conjunct his bride's progressed Ascendant at 19 degrees of Sagittarius. She had her progressed Part of Fortune at 18 degrees of Gemini, one degree from his natal Descendant.

Part of Fortune to Midheaven or IC

Conjunctions, sextiles, or trines to these points—natal, progressed, or converse—are also common. Marie W. had her progressed Part of Fortune conjunct her own progressed Midheaven at the time of marriage. Her husband Jim had his converse Part of Fortune trine his wife's converse Midheaven on the same date. This must have been a wedding where the bride was particularly radiant and in the limelight. I know it was a big wedding; they didn't elope.

Part of Fortune to Sun, Moon, Venus, or Mars

When you look back at the month a couple married, you'll often find that these planets were in conjunction or in trine or sextile to the progressed or converse Part of Fortune. Your progressed Part of Fortune may be conjunct your own natal, progressed, or converse Sun, while in trine to a partner's Venus or Mars. In addition to the Midheaven aspects described above, Marie and Jim W. also had these aspects going for them on their wedding date. Her progressed Part of Fortune was conjunct his Mars, while her converse Part of Fortune was conjunct her own natal Venus. His progressed Part of Fortune was conjunct her Sun.

Part of Fortune to the Part of Marriage

This is an interesting aspect which I have seen quite a few times in marriage charts. The aspect has usually been to one's own Part of Marriage rather than to the partner's, however. Most often the progressed or converse Part of Fortune has exactly conjoined one's natal Part of Marriage. This, naturally, is a very significant aspect when seen along with other marriage aspects.

Part of Fortune to Other Planets in the Chart

Although the aspects described above are the ones I have most frequently seen in charts at the time of marriage, there is sometimes a conjunction to some other planet in one's own or a mate's chart. Jupiter and Saturn lead in this regard. This is particularly true when one of these planets rules or occupies the seventh house of marriage.

The Part of Fascination as a Marriage Timer

A conjunction of one person's Part of Fascination to the other's significant planet seems a vital indication of the kind of interest between two people that can lead to marriage. This is how the Part of Fascination described the marriage of Ned and Elaine W.

Natally, their Parts of Fascination didn't form strongly significant conjunctions to planets in each other's charts. This may have been one of the reasons for their subsequent divorce. The year these two met and married, however, the fascination must have been strong. Her progressed Part of Fascination was at 23 degrees of Gemini conjunct his converse Part of Fascination. In both charts, these Parts of Fascination accompanied marriage aspects.

Her converse Moon was also at 23 degrees of Gemini the month they married, and this was conjunct her first-house North Node at 23 degrees of Gemini. In trine to this large conjunction was her marriage-house ruler, Jupiter, in her fifth house of romance, at 23 degrees of Libra. This was a definite marriage timer for the month.

His converse Part of Fascination fell in his third house at 23 degrees of Gemini, and it was trine to his progressed Mercury at 23 degrees of Libra in his seventh house of marriage. His ideas about getting married were right in tune with hers!

In examining many charts at the time of marriage, I have seen the Part of Fascination often a factor.

The Part of Karma as a Marriage Timer

The Part of Karma also seems to be an active link between charts at the time of marriage. Remember that this is the Arabic Part that indicates possible past-life involvement. It also seems to denote a scenario in which some issue from the past must be resolved through the interactions of the partnership.

Although you can progress the Part of Karma, it does not tend to move too far from its natal position in the progressed or converse charts—usually it is only a matter of a few degrees. This is because of the fairly constant similarity of speed between the Ascendant and Sun, and the fact that progressed and converse Saturns do not move far from natal places.

Because of this, it's usually enough to look for aspects that move into orb of the natal Part of Karma. These will most frequently be made from one partner's progressed or converse Descendant, Midheaven, Moon, Sun, or Jupiter to the other's natal Part of Karma. But any of the planets or angles of the other's chart may be involved, although not quite as frequently. Even conjunctions of one person's natal Part of Karma to the other's progressed or converse Arabic Parts have been noted at the time of marriage, particularly to the fast-moving Part of Fortune.

An example of a seemingly very fated union that changed many lives is that of the Duke and Duchess of Windsor. When he gave up his British throne in 1936 to marry the American divorcée, Wallis Simpson, he shocked the world. Needless to say, there were indications in their birth charts of a karmic connection. Simpson's natal Part of Karma was around 2 degrees of Cancer. This was conjunct

149

Edward's Sun at 2 degrees of Cancer. The timer to this connection was her converse Descendant arriving at 2 degrees of Cancer.

Edward's natal Part of Karma at 19 degrees of Taurus became strongly activated by one of Mrs. Simpson's significant marriage aspects the year that he gave up his throne to marry her. The degree of 19 degrees of Taurus just happened to be the position of both her progressed Mars and converse Sun. As you'll recall from past chapters, a Sun/Mars combination is a very potent marriage aspect in a woman's chart. It was a fateful combination.

Another example: When Jane Wyman married Ronald Reagan, her natal Part of Karma at 17 degrees of Pisces was conjunct his progressed Sun at 16 degrees of Pisces.

Putting It All Together

There are a good many factors to consider if you really go into details about the pros and cons of a possible marriage time or partner, but it is well worth your efforts to attempt to see what the relationship is all about before you take the plunge.

Here's to your success in finding happiness through greater astrological understanding.

Computer Chart Services

1. Astro Computing Services
   P.O. Box 16430
   San Diego, CA 92116-0430
   (800) 826-1085

2. Astro Numeric Service
   P.O. Box 1020
   El Cerrito, CA 94530
   (415) 232-5572

3. Llewellyn's Personal Services
   (At the back of this book you will find an order form, a list of the types
   of astrological reports available, and a coupon offering 30% off the
   price of a compatibility profile.)
   P.O. Box 64383-K479
   St. Paul, MN 55164-0383
   (612) 291-1970

Appendix B

List of Sources
for Birthchart
Data

From *Profiles of Women*, Lois Rodden, A.F.A., Tempe, AZ, 1979.

   Browning, Elizabeth Barrett
   Davies, Marion
   Diana, Princess of Wales
   Farrow, Mia
   Fitzgerald, Zelda
   Gardner, Ava
   Gwyn, Nell
   Lombard, Carole
   MacDonald, Jeanette
   Marie Antoinette

Simpson, Wallis, Duchess of Windsor
Taylor, Elizabeth
Villiers, Barbara
Woodward, Joanne

From *American Book of Charts*, Lois Rodden, ACS, 1990.

Burton, Richard
Charles, Prince of Wales
Fitzgerald, F. Scott
Gable, Clark
Newman, Paul
Todd, Mike
Windsor, Duke of

From *Interpreting Your Sun-Ascendant*, Joan McEvers, Astro-Analytics Publications, 1980.

Browning, Robert
Eddy, Nelson
Hearst, William Randolph

From *Astrology in Action*, Marcia Moore and Mark Douglas, Arcane Publications, 1970.

Kennedy, John
Onassis, Jacqueline Kennedy

From *Astrology in Action*, Paul Wright, CRCS, 1989.

Allen, Woody
Charles II, England

From *Notable Nativities*, Aries Press, Chicago.

Louis XVI, France #693

From *An Astrological Who's Who*, Marc Penfield, Arcane Publications, 1972.

Sinatra, Frank

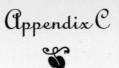

Appendix C

Celebrity
Charts

Allen, Woody 160

Astaire, Fred 186

Astaire, Robyn Smyth 187

Browning, Elizabeth Barrett 161

Browning, Robert 162

Burton, Richard 157–8

Charles, Prince 163

Charles II, King 164

Davies, Marion 159

Diana, Princess of Wales 165

Duchess of Windsor 166

Duke of Windsor 167

Eddy, Nelson 168

Farrow, Mia 169

Fitzgerald, F. Scott 170

Fitzgerald, Zelda 171

Gable, Clark 172

Gardner, Ava 173

Gwyn, Nell 174

Hearst, William Randolph 159

Kennedy, John F. 175

Lombard, Carole 176, 185

Louis XVI of France 177

Marie Antoinette 178

MacDonald, Jeanette 179

Newman, Paul 180

Simpson, Wallis (Duchess of Windsor) 166

Sinatra, Frank 181

Smyth, Robyn (Astaire) 187

Taylor, Elizabeth 157–8

Todd, Mike 182

Triple-wheel examples 185–7

Villiers, Barbara 183

Woodward, Joanne 184

156

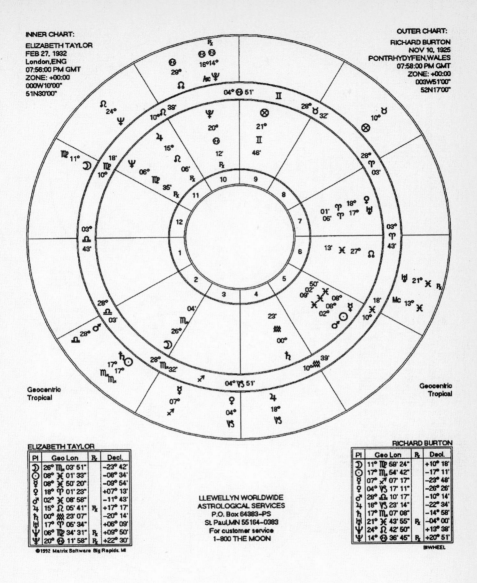

LLEWELLYN WORLDWIDE
ASTROLOGICAL SERVICES
P.O. Box 64383–PS
St. Paul, MN 55164–0383
For customer service
1–800 THE MOON

©1992 Matrix Software Big Rapids, MI

Inner Wheel, Elizabeth Taylor: February 27, 1932, 7:56 PM Greenwich Mean Time, London, England.

Outer Wheel, Richard Burton: November 10, 1925, 7:58 PM Greenwich Mean Time, Pontrhydyfen, Wales.

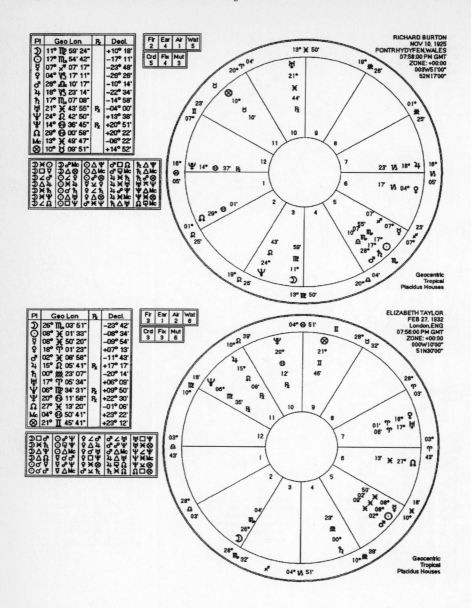

Top Chart, Richard Burton: November 10, 1925, 7:58 PM Greenwich Mean Time, Pontrhydyfen, Wales.

Lower Chart, Elizabeth Taylor: February 27, 1932, 7:56 PM Greenwich Mean Time, London, England.

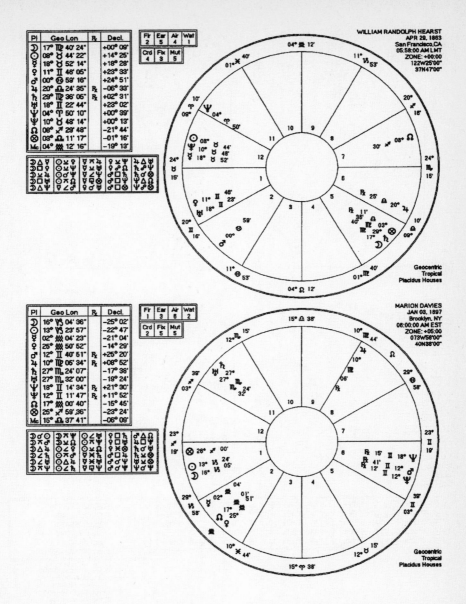

Top Chart, William Randolph Hearst: April 29, 1863, 5:58 AM Local Mean Time, San Francisco, California.

Lower Chart, Marion Davies: January 3, 1897, 6:00 AM Eastern Standard Time, Brooklyn, New York.

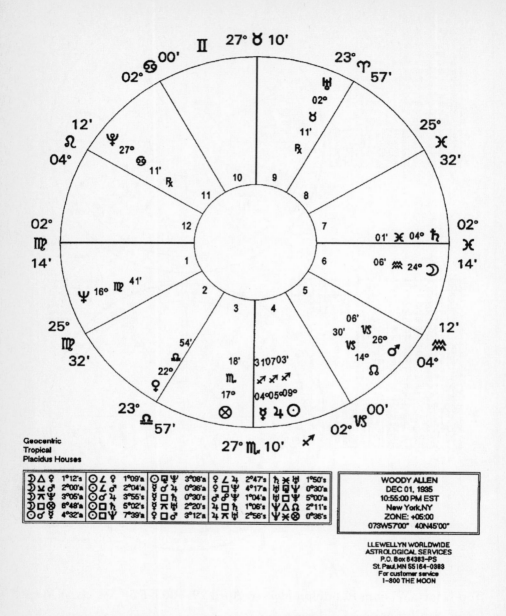

Geocentric
Tropical
Placidus Houses

WOODY ALLEN
DEC 01, 1935
10:55:00 PM EST
New York,NY
ZONE: +05:00
073W57'00" 40N45'00"

LLEWELLYN WORLDWIDE
ASTROLOGICAL SERVICES
P.O. Box 64383–PS
St. Paul,MN 55164–0383
For customer service
1–800 THE MOON

Woody Allen: December 1, 1935, 10:55 PM Eastern Standard Time, New York City, New York.

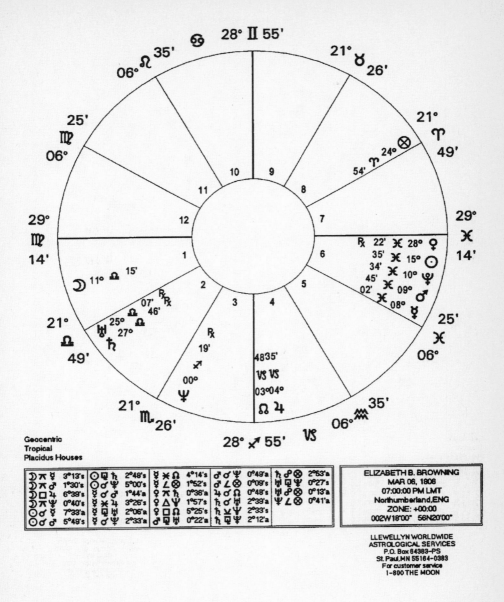

Geocentric
Tropical
Placidus Houses

ELIZABETH B. BROWNING
MAR 06, 1806
07:00:00 PM LMT
Northumberland,ENG
ZONE: +00:00
002W18'00" 56N20'00"

LLEWELLYN WORLDWIDE
ASTROLOGICAL SERVICES
P.O. Box 64383-PS
St. Paul,MN 55164-0383
For customer service
1-800 THE MOON

Elizabeth Barrett Browning: March 6, 1806, 7:00 PM Local Mean Time,
Northumberland, England.

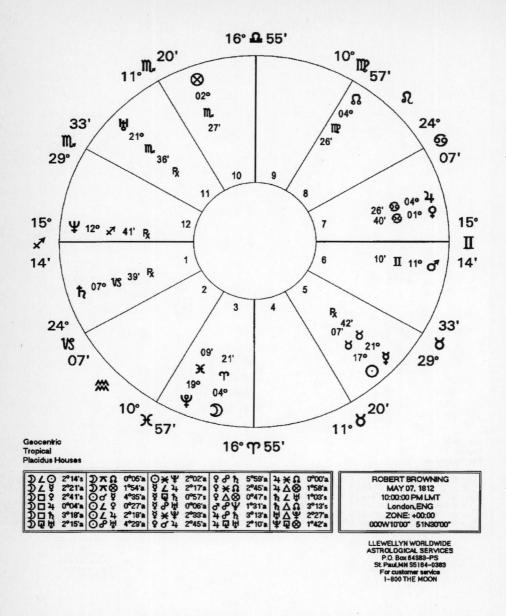

Robert Browning: May 7, 1812, 10:00 PM Local Mean Time, London, England.

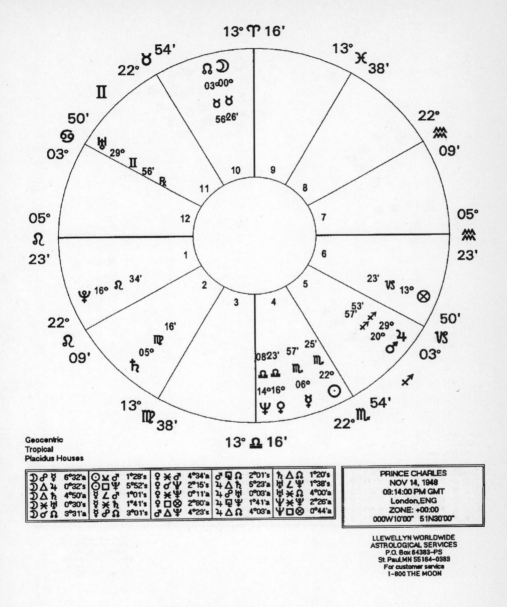

Geocentric
Tropical
Placidus Houses

Prince Charles: November 14, 1948, 9:14 PM Greenwich Mean Time, London, England.

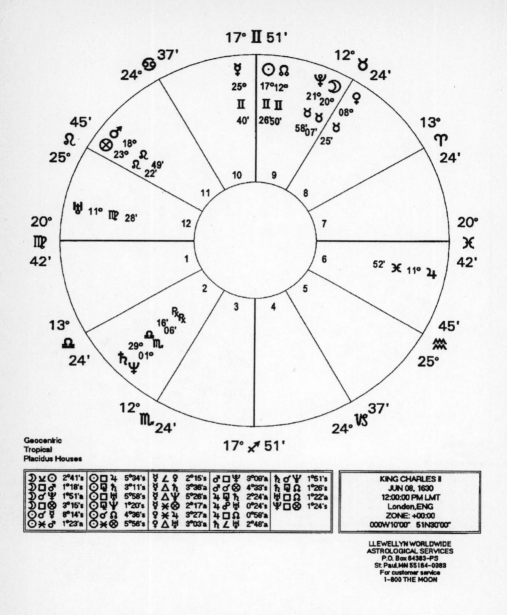

Geocentric
Tropical
Placidus Houses

KING CHARLES II
JUN 08, 1630
12:00:00 PM LMT
London,ENG
ZONE: +00:00
000W10'00" 51N30'00"

LLEWELLYN WORLDWIDE
ASTROLOGICAL SERVICES
P.O. Box 64383-PS
St. Paul, MN 55164-0383
For customer service
1-800 THE MOON

King Charles II: June 8, 1630, 12:00 PM Local Mean Time, London, England.

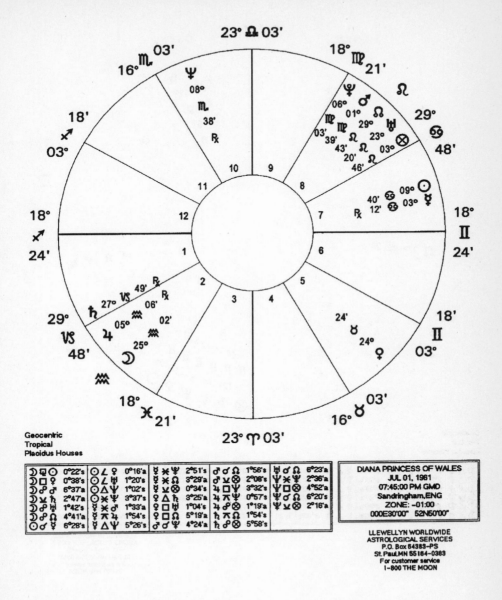

Diana, Princess of Wales: July 1, 1961, 7:45 PM Greenwich Daylight Time,
Sandringham, England.

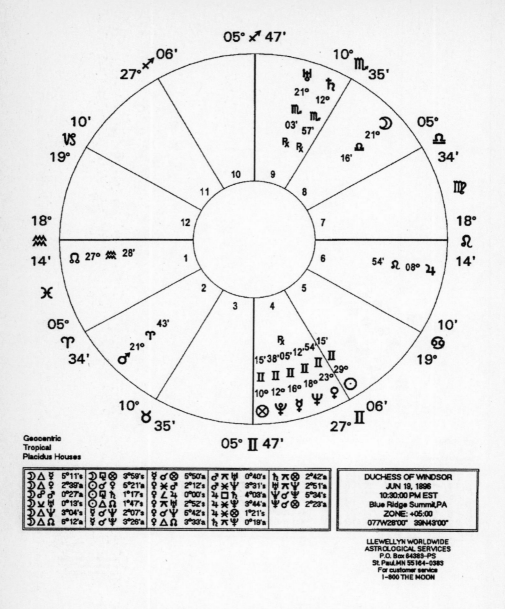

Geocentric
Tropical
Placidus Houses

Duchess of Windsor (Wallis Simpson): June 19, 1896, 10:30 PM Eastern
Standard Time, Blue Ridge Summit, Pennsylvania.

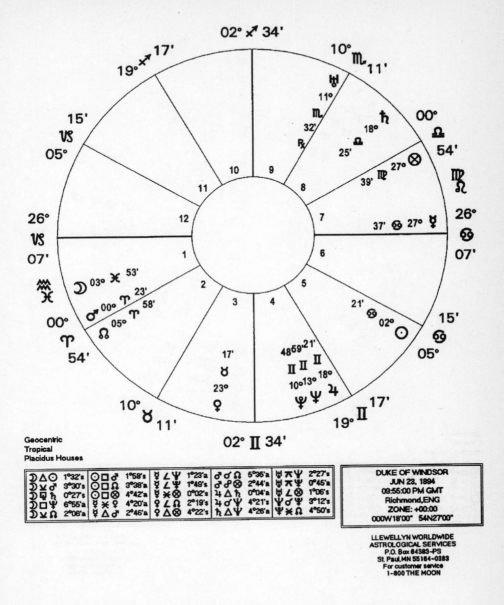

Geocentric
Tropical
Placidus Houses

DUKE OF WINDSOR
JUN 23, 1894
09:55:00 PM GMT
Richmond,ENG
ZONE: +00:00
000W18'00" 54N27'00"

LLEWELLYN WORLDWIDE
ASTROLOGICAL SERVICES
P.O. Box 64383-PS
St. Paul, MN 55164-0383
For customer service
1-800 THE MOON

Duke of Windsor: June 23, 1894, 9:55 PM Greenwich Mean Time, Richmond, England.

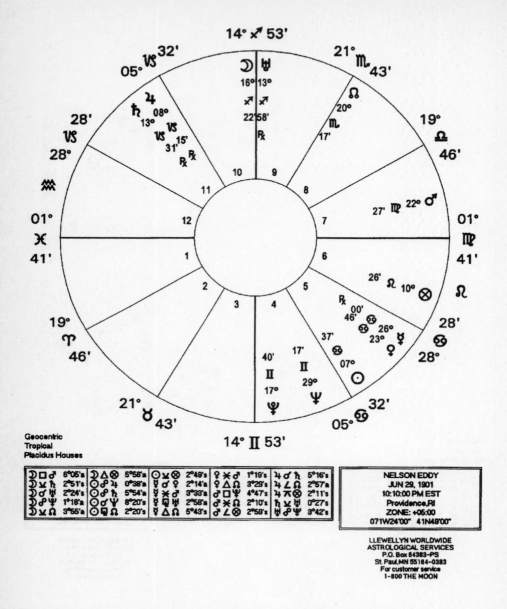

Geocentric
Tropical
Placidus Houses

☽□♂	6°05'a	☽△⊗	5°58'a	☉⚷⊗	2°49's	♀⚹♂	1°19's	♃♂♄	5°16's
☽⚹♄	2°51's	☉♂♃	0°38'a	☉♂♀	2°14'a	♀□♂	3°29's	♃∠☊	2°57a
☽♂♅	2°24's	☉♂♄	5°54'a	☿⚹⊗	3°33'a	♂□♆	4°47's	♃π⊗	2°11's
☽⚹♆	1°18'a	☉♂♅	8°20's	☿⚼♀	2°58's	♂⚹☊	2°10's	♄∠♆	0°27's
☽⚹☊	3°55'a	☉□☊	2°20's	☿△☊	5°43's	♂∠⊗	2°58's	♅♂♆	3°42's

NELSON EDDY
JUN 29, 1901
10:10:00 PM EST
Providence,RI
ZONE: +05:00
071W24'00" 41N49'00"

LLEWELLYN WORLDWIDE
ASTROLOGICAL SERVICES
P.O. Box 64383-PS
St. Paul,MN 55164-0383
For customer service
1-800 THE MOON

Nelson Eddy: June 29, 1901, 10:10 PM Eastern Standard Time, Providence, Rhode Island.

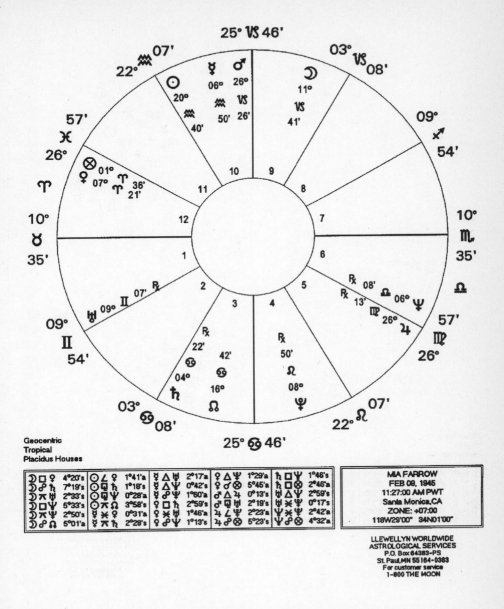

Geocentric
Tropical
Placidus Houses

MIA FARROW
FEB 09, 1945
11:27:00 AM PWT
Santa Monica, CA
ZONE: +07:00
118W29'00" 34N01'00"

LLEWELLYN WORLDWIDE
ASTROLOGICAL SERVICES
P.O. Box 64383-PS
St. Paul, MN 55164-0383
For customer service
1-800 THE MOON

Mia Farrow: February 9, 1945, 11:27 AM Pacific War Time, Santa Monica, California.

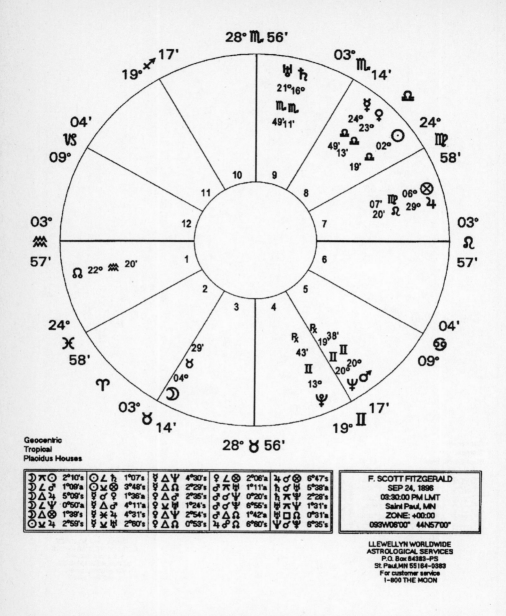

Geocentric
Tropical
Placidus Houses

☽ π ☉	2°10's	☉ ∠ ♄	1°07's	☿ △ ♇	4°30's	♀ ∠ ⊗	2°06'a	♃ ♂ ⊗	6°47's
☽ ∠ ♂	1°09'a	☉ ✶ ⊗	3°48's	☿ △ ♑	2°29's	♀ ∠ ♃	1°11'a	♄ ♂ ♆	5°38'a
☽ △ ♃	5°09's	☉ ♂ ♀	1°36'a	☿ △ ♆	2°35's	♂ ♂ ♆	0°20's	♄ π ♀	2°28's
☽ ∠ ♅	0°50'a	☿ △ ♂	4°11'a	♀ ✶ ♅	1°24's	♂ ♂ ♀	6°55's	♅ π ♀	1°31's
☽ △ ⊗	1°39's	☿ ✶ ♃	4°31's	♀ △ ♆	2°54's	♃ △ ♑	1°42's	♅ □ ♀	0°31's
☉ ✶ ♃	2°59's	☿ □ ♅	2°60's	♀ △ ♑	0°53's	♃ ♂ ♑	6°60's	♇ ∨ ♀	6°35's

F. SCOTT FITZGERALD
SEP 24, 1896
03:30:00 PM LMT
Saint Paul, MN
ZONE: +00:00
093W06'00" 44N5700"

LLEWELLYN WORLDWIDE
ASTROLOGICAL SERVICES
P.O. Box 64383-PS
St. Paul, MN 55164-0383
For customer service
1-800 THE MOON

F. Scott Fitzgerald: September 24, 1896, 3:30 PM Local Mean Time, St. Paul, Minnesota.

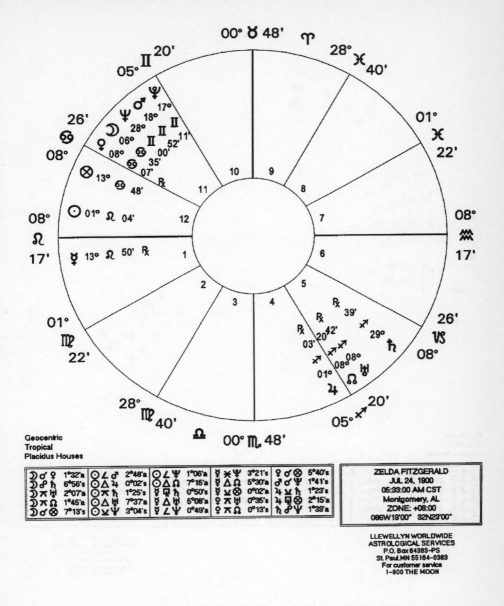

Zelda Fitzgerald: July 24, 1900, 5:33 AM Central Standard Time, Montgomery, Alabama.

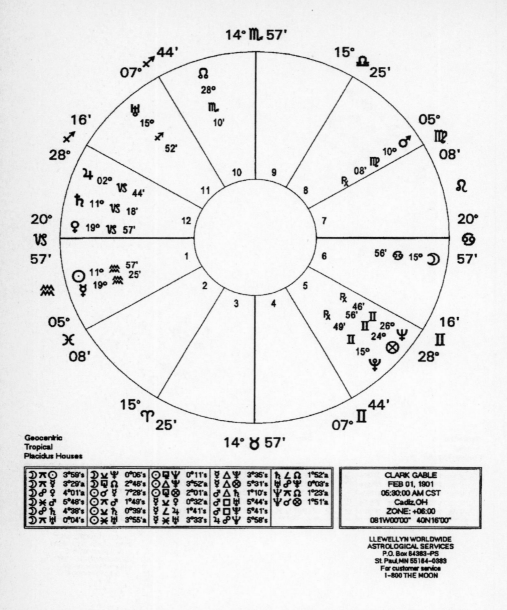

Geocentric
Tropical
Placidus Houses

CLARK GABLE
FEB 01, 1901
05:30:00 AM CST
Cadiz, OH
ZONE: +06:00
081W00'00" 40N16'00"

Clark Gable: February 1, 1901, 5:30 AM Central Standard Time, Cadiz, Ohio.

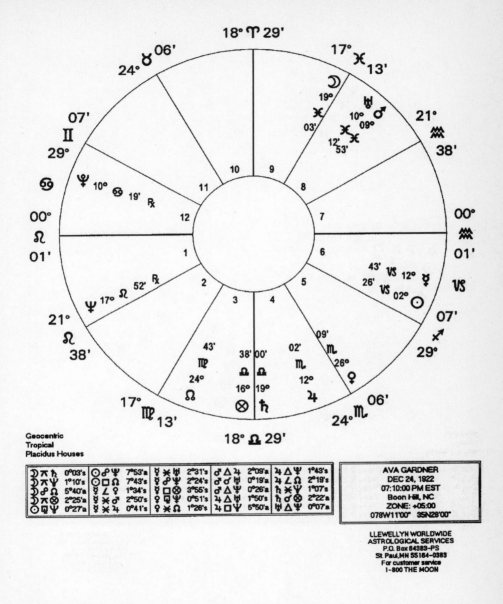

18° ♈ 29'

24° ♉ 06'

17° ♓ 13'

07'
♊
29°

☽ 19°
♓ 03'

♅ 10°
♂ 09°

♓ 12° 53'

21°
♒
38'

00°
♌
01'

♆ 10° ⊕ 19° ℞

11

10   9

8

00°
♒
01'

♇ 17° ♌ 52' ℞

12   1   2   3   4   5   6   7

43' ♑ 12° ☿
26' ♑ 02° ☉

♑

21°
♌
38'

43'
♍ 24° ♌

38' 00'
♎ ♎
16° 19°
⊗ ♄

02'
♏ 12°
♃

09'
♏ 26°
♀

07'
♐
29°

17°
♍ 13'

18° ♎ 29'

24° ♏ 06'

Geocentric
Tropical
Placidus Houses

☽ π ♄	0°03's	☉ ⚹ ♆	7°53'a	☿ ⚹ ♅	2°31's	♂ △ ♃	2°09'a	♃ △ ♆	1°43's
☽ π ♇	1°10's	☉ □ ♇	7°43's	☿ □ ♇	2°24's	♂ ♂ ♅	0°19'a	♃ ∠ ♇	2°19's
☽ ♂ ♇	5°40'a	☿ ∠ ♆	1°34's	☿ □ ♇	3°55's	♂ △ ♆	0°26'a	♄ ⚹ ♅	1°07's
☽ π ⊗	2°25'a	☿ ⚹ ♂	2°50's	♀ ⚹ ♇	0°51's	♃ △ ♅	1°50's	♄ ⊗ ♇	2°22'a
☉ □ ♇	0°27a	☿ ⚹ ♃	0°41's	♀ ⚹ ♀	1°26's	♃ □ ♀	5°50's	♃ △ ♆	0°07'a

AVA GARDNER
DEC 24, 1922
07:10:00 PM EST
Boon Hill, NC
ZONE: +05:00
078W11'00" 35N28'00"

LLEWELLYN WORLDWIDE
ASTROLOGICAL SERVICES
P.O. Box 84383-PS
St. Paul, MN 55164-0383
For customer service
1-800 THE MOON

Ava Gardner: December 24, 1922, 7:10 PM Eastern Standard Time, Boon Hill Township, North Carolina.

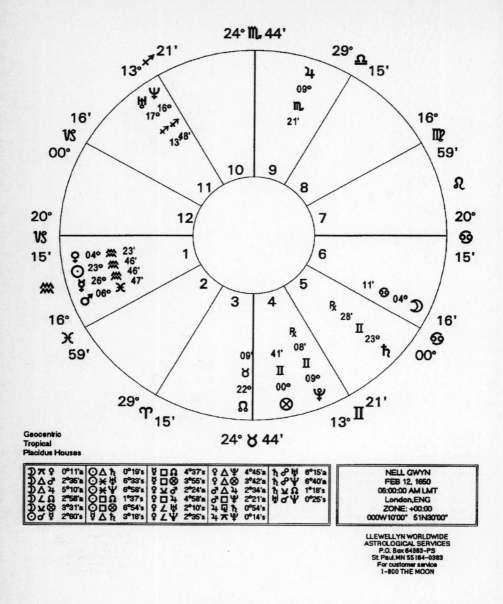

Geocentric
Tropical
Placidus Houses

☽ ⚹ ♀	0°11'a	☉ △ ♄	0°19's	☿ □ ♅	4°37's	♀ △ ♆	4°45'a	♄ ☌ ♃	6°15's
☽ △ ♂	2°35'a	☉ ⚹ ♅	6°33's	☿ □ ♆	3°55's	♀ △ ⊗	3°42's	♄ ⚹ ♇	6°40'a
☽ △ ♃	5°10'a	☉ ⚹ ♆	6°58's	♀ ☌ ♂	2°24's	♂ △ ♃	2°34's	♄ ⚺ ☊	1°18's
☽ ⚺ ♄	2°58's	☉ □ ♇	1°37's	♀ △ ♆	4°58'a	♂ ⚹ ♇	2°21's	♅ ⚼ ♇	0°25's
☉ ⚺ ♀	3°31's	☉ □ ⊗	6°54's	♀ ☌ ♃	2°10's	♃ □ ♄	0°54's		
☉ ☌ ♂	2°60's	☿ △ ♄	3°18's	♀ ⚺ ♆	2°35's	♃ ⚻ ♆	0°14's		

NELL GWYN
FEB 12, 1650
06:00:00 AM LMT
London,ENG
ZONE: +00:00
000W10'00" 51N30'00"

LLEWELLYN WORLDWIDE
ASTROLOGICAL SERVICES
P.O. Box 64383-PS
St. Paul, MN 55164-0383
For customer service
1-800 THE MOON

Nell Gwyn: February 12, 1650, 6:00 AM Local Mean Time, London, England.

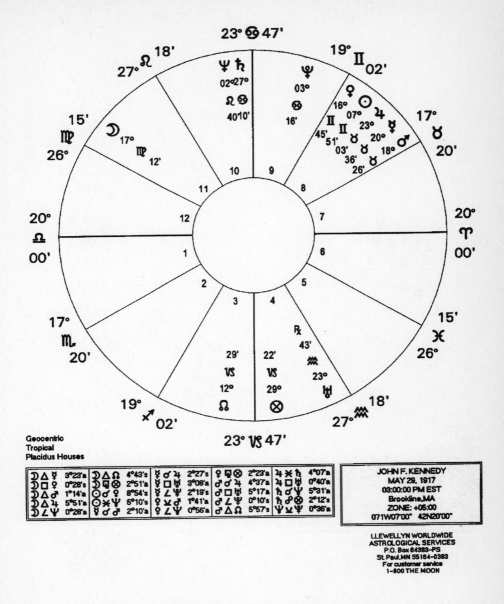

JOHN F. KENNEDY
MAY 29, 1917
03:00:00 PM EST
Brookline, MA
ZONE: +05:00
071W07'00" 42N20'00"

LLEWELLYN WORLDWIDE
ASTROLOGICAL SERVICES
P.O. Box 64383-PS
St. Paul, MN 55164-0383
For customer service
1-800 THE MOON

John F. Kennedy: May 29, 1917, 3:00 PM Eastern Standard Time, Brookline, Massachusetts.

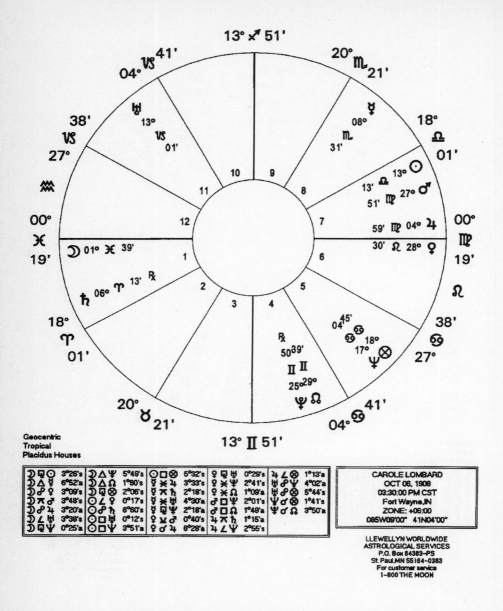

Carole Lombard: October 6, 1908, 3:30 PM Central Standard Time, Fort Wayne, Indiana.

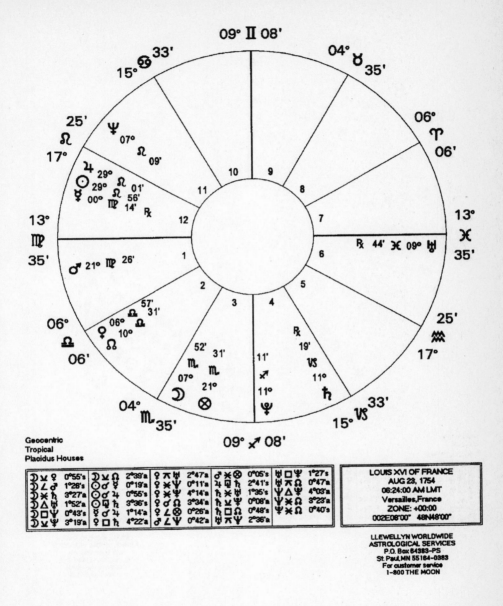

Louis XVI of France: August 23, 1754, 6:24 AM Local Mean Time, Versailles, France.

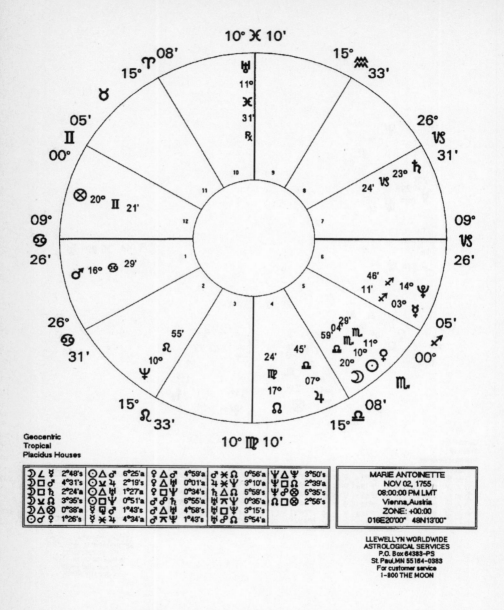

Marie Antoinette, November 2, 1755, 8:00 PM Local Mean Time, Vienna, Austria.

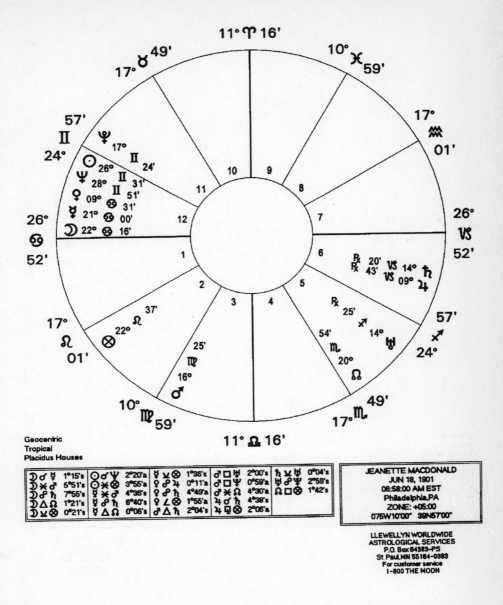

Geocentric
Tropical
Placidus Houses

☽ ♂ ☿	1°15's	☉ ♂ ♆	2°20'a	♀ ⚹ ⊗	1°36's	♂ □ ♆	2°00's	♄ ⚹ ⛢	0°04's
☽ ⚹ ☿	5°51's	☉ ⚹ ⊗	3°55'a	♀ ⚹ ♄	4°49'a	♂ □ ♆	0°59'a	⛢ ♀ ⊗	2°59's
☽ ⚹ ♄	7°55's	☉ ⚹ ♄	4°36'a	♀ ⚹ ♄	4°49'a	♂ ⚹ ♆	4°30'a	☊ □ ⊗	1°42's
☽ △ ☊	1°21's	♀ ♂ ♆	6°40's	♀ ∠	1°55's	♃ ♂ ♄	4°38's		
☽ ⚹ ⊗	0°21's	☿ △ ☊	0°06's	♂ △ ♄	2°04's	♃ ♂ ⊗	2°06'a		

JEANETTE MACDONALD
JUN 18, 1901
06:58:00 AM EST
Philadelphia,PA
ZONE: +05:00
075W10'00" 39N57'00"

LLEWELLYN WORLDWIDE
ASTROLOGICAL SERVICES
P.O. Box 64383-PS
St. Paul,MN 55164-0383
For customer service
1-800 THE MOON

Jeanette MacDonald: June 18, 1901, 6:58 AM Eastern Standard Time,
Philadelphia, Pennsylvania.

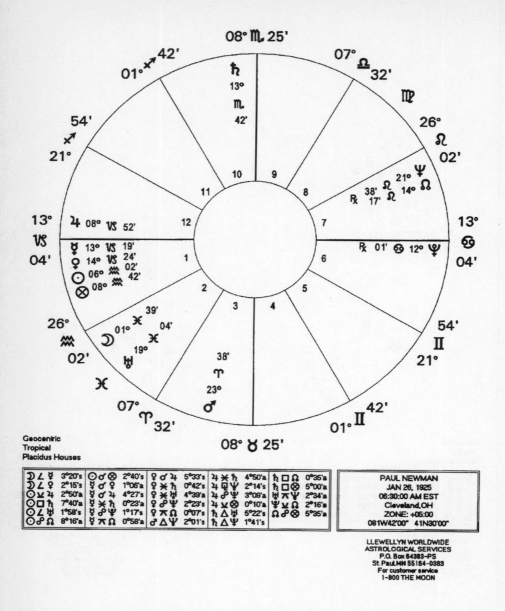

Geocentric
Tropical
Placidus Houses

PAUL NEWMAN
JAN 26, 1925
06:30:00 AM EST
Cleveland,OH
ZONE: +05:00
081W42'00" 41N30'00"

LLEWELLYN WORLDWIDE
ASTROLOGICAL SERVICES
P.O. Box 64383-PS
St. Paul,MN 55164-0383
For customer service
1-800 THE MOON

Paul Newman: January 26, 1925, 6:30 AM Eastern Standard Time, Cleveland, Ohio.

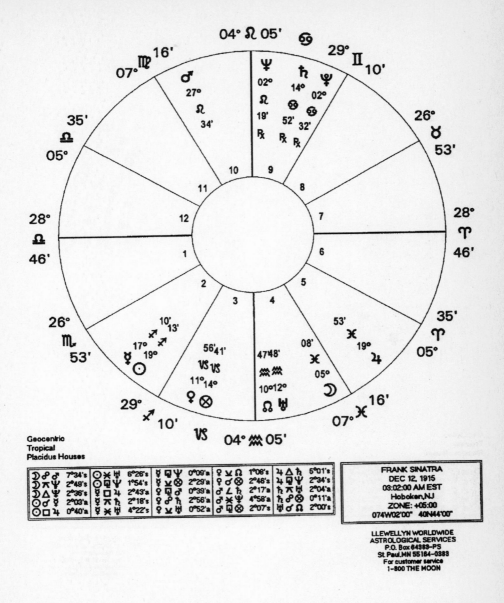

Geocentric
Tropical
Placidus Houses

FRANK SINATRA
DEC 12, 1915
03:02:00 AM EST
Hoboken, NJ
ZONE: +05:00
074W02'00" 40N44'00"

LLEWELLYN WORLDWIDE
ASTROLOGICAL SERVICES
P.O. Box 64383-PS
St. Paul, MN 55164-0383
For customer service
1-800 THE MOON

Frank Sinatra: December 12, 1915, 3:02 AM Eastern Standard Time, Hoboken, New Jersey.

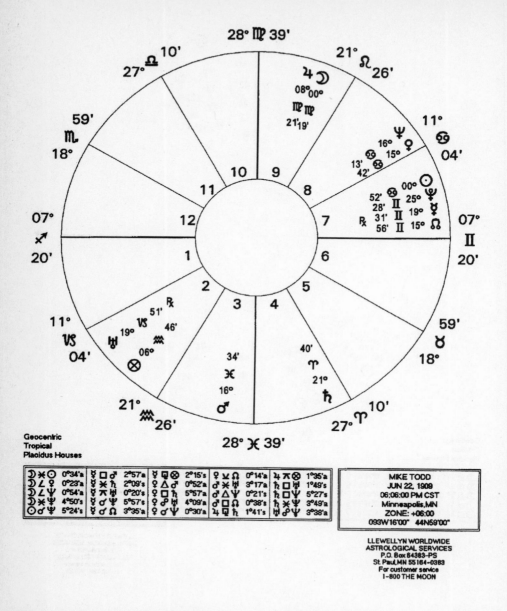

Mike Todd: June 22, 1909, 6:06 PM Central Standard Time, Minneapolis, Minnesota.

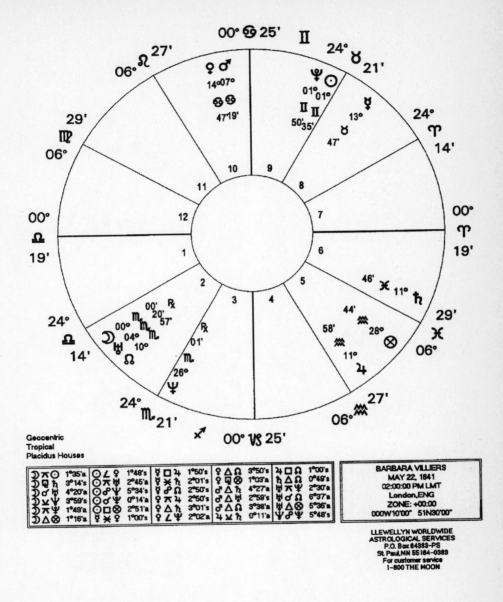

Geocentric
Tropical
Placidus Houses

BARBARA VILLIERS
MAY 22, 1641
02:00:00 PM LMT
London,ENG
ZONE: +00:00
000W10'00" 51N30'00"

LLEWELLYN WORLDWIDE
ASTROLOGICAL SERVICES
P.O. Box 64383-PS
St. Paul,MN 55164-0383
For customer service
1-800 THE MOON

Barbara Villiers: May 22, 1641, 2:00 PM Local Mean Time, London, England.

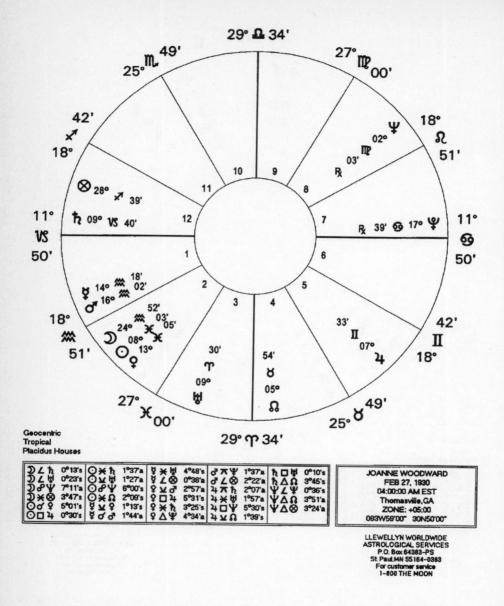

Geocentric
Tropical
Placidus Houses

☽∠♄ 0°13's	☉⚹♄ 1°37'a	☿⚹♅ 4°48's	♂⚼♆ 1°37'a	♄□♅ 0°10's
☽∠♅ 0°23's	☉⚼♅ 1°27'a	☿∠⊗ 0°38'a	♂∠⊗ 2°22'a	♄△☊ 3°45's
☽☌♇ 7°11'a	☉⚼♇ 6°00's	☿⚼♂ 2°57'a	♃⚼♄ 2°07'a	♄∠♃ 0°36's
☽⚹⊗ 3°47's	☉⚹☊ 2°09's	☿□♃ 5°31's	♃⚹♅ 1°57'a	♆△☊ 3°51's
☉♂♀ 5°01's	☉⚹♇ 1°13's	☿⚹♄ 3°25's	♃□♅ 5°30's	♆△⊗ 3°24'a
☉□♃ 0°30's	☿♂♀ 1°44'a	☿△♆ 4°34'a	♃⚼☊ 1°39's	

JOANNE WOODWARD
FEB 27, 1930
04:00:00 AM EST
Thomasville, GA
ZONE: +05:00
083W59'00" 30N50'00"

LLEWELLYN WORLDWIDE
ASTROLOGICAL SERVICES
P.O. Box 64383-PS
St. Paul,MN 55164-0383
For customer service
1-800 THE MOON

Joanne Woodward: February 27, 1930, 4:00 AM Eastern Standard Time, Thomasville, Georgia.

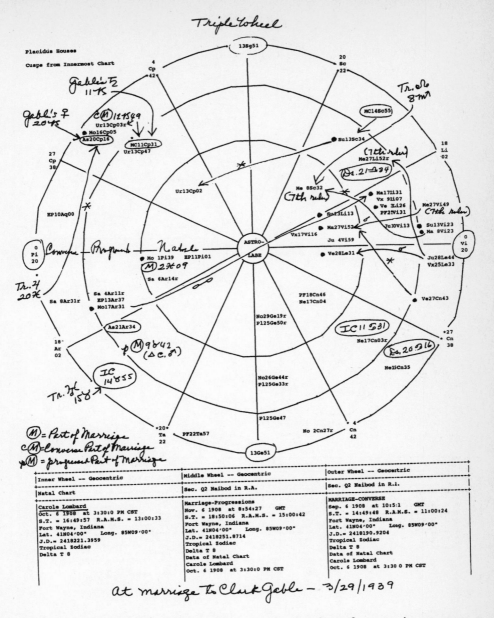

Triple Wheel

Example of author's triple-wheel comparison chart for marriage aspects: Carole Lombard's natal, progressed, and converse charts at time of marriage to Clark Gable March 29, 1939. Innermost wheel, natal; middle wheel, secondary progression; outer wheel, converse direction.

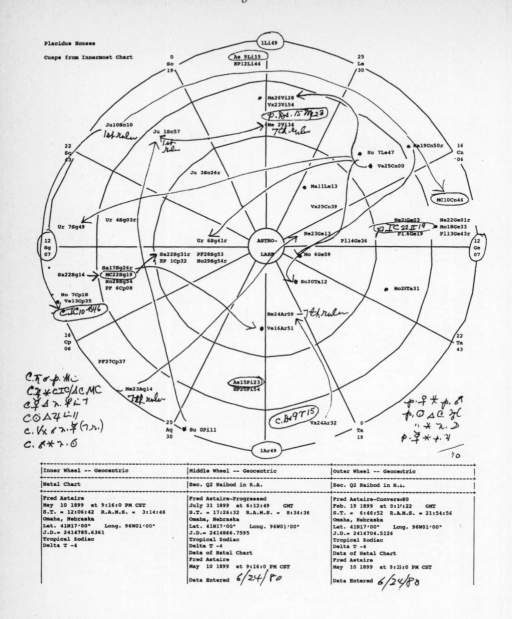

Example of author's triple-wheel comparison chart for marriage aspects: Fred Astaire's natal, progressed, and converse charts June 24, 1980. Innermost wheel, natal; middle wheel, secondary progression; outer wheel, converse direction.

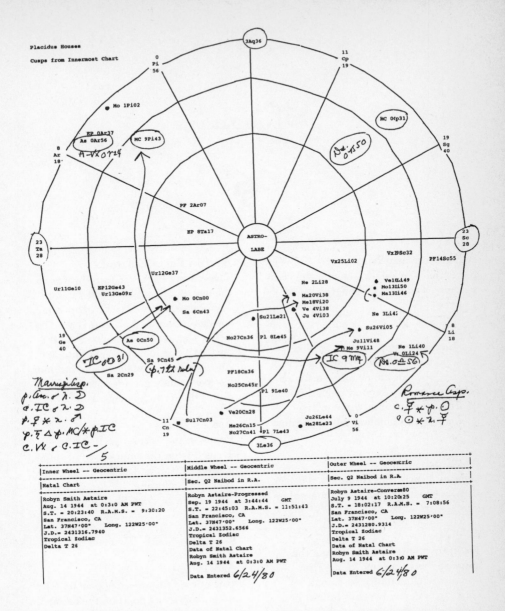

Example of author's triple-wheel comparison chart for marriage aspects: Robyn Smyth Astaire's natal, progressed, and converse charts June 24, 1980. Innermost wheel, natal; middle wheel, secondary progression; outer wheel, converse direction.

Glossary

Adjoining Sun Signs
Signs that are side-by-side in the zodiac. See "Zodiacal Order" for list of signs.

Afflict
A planet, especially Mars, Saturn, Uranus, Neptune, or Pluto, that is in square, opposition, or other difficult relationship to a second planet, is said to afflict the second planet, often accompanying challenging conditions in the life.

Air Signs
Gemini, Libra, and Aquarius. These signs are also known as the mental or intellectual signs.

Angles
The four points in a horoscope that indicate the beginning of the first house, or Ascendant; the fourth house, or IC; the seventh house, or Descendant; and the tenth house, or Midheaven.

Aquarius
See "Signs."

Arabic Parts Formula
The Arabic Parts are found through the use of a formula which can be symbolized as A + B - C. Most often, the Ascendant is A, B and C may be either planets or points, such as the cusp of a house. (Note: the Sun and Moon, which are technically luminaries, are usually grouped in astrology under the term "planets.")

Arabic Parts
Points in the horoscope that are derived from the interaction of three planets or points. Used by the ancients, including the Arabs. See "Arabic Parts Formula."

Aries
See "Signs."

Ascendant
One of the four angles of a chart. The Ascendant is the point on the eastern horizon which is also called the rising sign. It is the cusp (or beginning) of the first house. The sign on the Ascendant, and its ruling planet, describe something about the native's personal appearance and characteristics. It is the

Ascendant (cont.)
point in the chart which rules the person born at that time, while the opposite point, the Descendant, describes the kind of partner one may attract.

Aspect
One planet is in aspect to another when there is a precise number of degrees between them. The major aspects are the conjunction, sextile, square, trine, and opposition.

Benefic Planets
Favorable planets. According to ancient astrologers, Jupiter was known as the "greater benefic" and Venus as the "lesser benefic."

Birth Chart
A horoscope set up for the date, time, and place of birth.

Birth Data
The date and year of birth, the exact time, and the city, state, or country. This information is needed by an astrologer in order to set up a birth chart or horoscope.

Cancer
See "Signs."

Capricorn
See "Signs."

Challenging Aspects
Aspects such as the square, opposition, quincunx, semisquare, and sesquisquare.

Chart
Usually this refers to a birth chart. But it may also refer to a progressed chart, or to any chart for any event that an astrologer draws up in order to gain more information.

Co-Ruling, Co-Ruler
When there is an intercepted sign within the house of a chart, the planetary ruler of the intercepted sign also tells us something about that house and its affairs. See "Intercepted Sign."

Compatibility
In astrology, this is a term often used to signify how well one sign or person gets along with another sign or person. Certain signs are supposed to be more compatible than others. Generally, the Fire and Air signs get along with each other, and the Earth and Water signs are compatible with each other.

Composite Sun/Moon Midpoint
The zodiacal point half-way between one person's Sun/Moon midpoint and another person's Sun/Moon midpoint. See "Sun/Moon Midpoint."

Conjoined, Conjunct, Conjunction
All of these terms refer to planets or points which are close together by degree in the zodiac.

Converse Directions
Just the opposite of progressed planets. Instead of counting forward in the ephemeris from the birthdate one day for each year of life, one counts backwards from the date of birth; each day before birth is also equal to one year of life. In combination with the natal chart and progressions, these are useful in finding marriage indications for the current year.

Conversion Table
In order to add or subtract with degrees or to find midpoints, it's usually wise to convert the sign and degree of each planet to a 360-degree

Conversion Table (cont.)

wheel. Take the signs in zodiacal order and set up a conversion table in which 0 to 29 degrees of Aries equates with the numbers 0 to 29; in like manner 0 to 29 degrees of Taurus equate with the numbers 30 to 59, and so on. Degrees in Pisces will complete the wheel, ranging from 330 to 359. After adding, subtracting, or finding a midpoint, you can change the degrees back to sign and degree with this conversion table.

Culminating

Arrival of a planet at the Mid-heaven (cusp of the tenth house) by progression or transit. Can also mean the completion of an aspect which has been approaching.

Cusp

An imaginary line which separates one house from another house or one sign from another sign. In this book, cusp is used primarily to indicate the beginning of each house in one's chart and the degree of the zodiac marked beside it. The sign on the cusp is particularly important because the planet that rules that sign has much importance to the affairs of the house under consideration.

Decanates

Each sign consists of 30 degrees of the zodiac circle. A decanate, or decan, results from further division of the sign into three 10-degree segments. Each decanate of a sign is ruled by a different planet. The first decanate of Aries, for example, is ruled by Mars; the second by the Sun, the third by Jupiter. These are the planetary rulers of the three fire signs, Aries, Leo, and Sagittarius.

Degree

A unit of measurement in astrology; the circle of the zodiac is divided into 360 degrees; each of the twelve signs contains 30 degrees.

Descendant

The point opposite the Ascendant or rising sign. It also is the cusp of the seventh house. This house pertains to the marriage partner.

Direct

Direct motion as opposed to retrograde motion of a planet. When a planet is direct in apparent motion, its effects seem to be more beneficial. The word can also be used as a verb, to direct a planet, or advance its position in the chart in the zodiac.

Direction

To move planets through the horoscope, usually according to a formula that equates one day in the ephemeris to one year of one's life.

Duads

The division of a sign into twelve segments or duads, each symbolic of one sign of the zodiac. The first duad, or 2-1/2 degrees of each sign, is generally the same as the sign itself, with succeeding 2-1/2 degree duads being ruled by the signs following in zodiacal order.

Earth Signs

Taurus, Virgo, and Capricorn. These are known as the practical signs.

Eastern Horizon

Another term for the degree rising in the east which is the cusp of the first house, also called the Ascendant.

Eclipse
A solar eclipse occurs when the Moon passes in front of the Sun at the time of a New Moon, cutting off some or all of the solar light. A lunar eclipse occurs at the time of a Full Moon and temporarily blots out a part or all of the Moon. In astrology, each eclipse is described by its zodiacal position. The house in one's natal chart in which the eclipse occurs is generally activated for a period of time after the eclipse.

Elements
Fire, Earth, Air, and Water; each of the signs of the zodiac is characterized by one of these. Fire and Air are harmonious to each other. Earth and Water are harmonious.

Ephemeris
An almanac containing planetary positions for each day of the year at noon or at midnight.

Falls On
Is conjunct to. In a similar sector or degree of the zodiac.

Favorable Aspects
Favorable distances between planets and points in the horoscope. These are the trine and the sextile, and, depending on the planets involved, also the conjunction.

Fire Signs
Aries, Leo, and Sagittarius. These are known as the inspirational signs.

Focal Point
Usually a planet at the midpoint of two or more other planets that influences the general meaning of the configuration.

Four Angles
See "Angles."

Gemini
See "Signs."

Grand Trine
A very favorable configuration of planets in a horoscope. This consists of three or more planets in trine or approximately 120 degrees from each other, forming a triangle. These planets are usually in signs of the same element. A grand trine can be completed by a planet from another's chart, making that person very lucky for you.

Grand Money Trine
A grand trine involving planets in or ruling your money houses. If you have a trine to one of your money planets, a person whose planet or planets form a third angle can be financially lucky for you.

Hard Aspects
Aspects between planets that are conjunct, square, opposed, semisquare, or sesquisquare.

Harmonious Aspects
Favorable distances between planets. They promote harmony and ease. The favorable aspects are: sextile, trine, and (usually) conjunct. The disharmonious aspects between planets are the square and opposition.

Horoscope
As generally used, this means the chart of the planets' places at a certain date, time, and place, such as a birth chart or horoscope. In modern times, this is usually shown in the form of a circle, divided into twelve houses, each symbolizing an area of one's life. See "Houses."

House Ruler
This refers to the planet
which rules the sign on the cusp
(beginning) of that house. See
"Rulers."

Houses
The twelve sections of the horoscope
ruling different areas of one's life. The
houses we are concerned with in this
book are the first, fifth, and seventh
for love and marriage indications, plus
the second and eighth for money compatibility. First house rules oneself,
second house rules one's money, earnings and possessions, fifth house rules
romance and children, seventh house
rules the marriage partner, and eighth
house rules the partner's money.

IC
An abbreviation for the Latin term,
Imum Coeli, the lowest point in the
horoscope, and one of the four angles.
It is the cusp of the fourth house.

In Aspect to
When we say that one planet is in
aspect to another, we mean that the
distance between these planets by
degree correlates to one of the recog-
nized aspects of astrology, such as the
conjunction, sextile, square, or trine.

Intercepted Signs
A sign is intercepted when it is wholly
contained within a house, and does
not appear on the cusp of that house
or the next house.

Jupiter
See "Planets."

Karmic Ties
Indications in the chart that ties were
formed in a former life that are still
influential in the current life.

Leo
See "Signs."

Libra
See "Signs."

Links
Planets or points that seem to link one
chart with another because of their
similarity.

Love Planets
Sun, Moon, Venus, and Mars.

Love Links
Aspects between charts that indicate
compatibility.

Lucky Trines
See "Trine."

Lunar Nodes
The point of the zodiac at which the
Moon crosses from the south into
north latitude is called the North
Node. The opposite point is termed
the South Node. The North Node is
generally thought to be more fortunate, while the South Node is believed
to symbolize what you brought from a
former life. Therefore, another's planets in combination with your South
Node may indicate that you knew that
person in a former life.

Marriage Year
A year when aspects form in your
chart that indicate the possibility of
marriage that year.

Marriage Ruler
The planet that rules the cusp of the
seventh house in your natal chart.

Marriage Aspects
Aspects between planets that indicate
the possibility of marriage.

Marriage Timer
A planet, point, or Part that
helps to indicate more precisely the
month or day of possible marriage.

Mars
See "Planets."

Midheaven
The cusp of the tenth house. It is one
of the four angles of a chart, important in timing marriage. Often abbre-
viated as MC.

Midpoint
The zodiacal degree that is half-way
between two other degrees.

Minor Aspects
In this book, the minor aspects used
are the semisquare and the sesquisquare. Also the quincunx (150°).

Money Planets
Those planets that occupy or rule the
money houses in one's natal chart,
especially the second and eighth houses. These indicate the good fortune, or
lack of it, in money matters shown at
birth.

Money Grand Trine
See "Grand Trine" and "Grand
Money Trine."

Moon
Although the Moon is the Earth's
satellite, in astrology it is commonly
grouped under the term "Planets." See
"Planets."

Moon's Nodes
See "Lunar Nodes."

Nadir
Also known as the IC or cusp of the
fourth house.

Natal
Indicates the type of chart or horoscope that is based upon the date,
time, and place of birth.

Native
In astrology, the subject of a chart or
horoscope, or one born under a certain sign.

Negative Aspects
Indications in a horoscope that there
is difficulty or challenge involved in
the alignment of the planets.

Neptune
See "Planets."

New Moon
The conjunction of the Sun and Moon.
In astrology, this conjunction general-
ly indicates a new start of some sort.

Nodal Connections
Aspects between one person's lunar
nodes and another's planets or points.

North Node
See "Lunar Nodes."

Opposed, Opposing, Opposition
A major aspect in astrology. Two
planets that oppose each other or form
an opposition symbolize a pulling
apart, but may also indicate a challenging attraction as when "opposites
attract."

Orb
Planets are in orb when they
are within a certain number of degrees
from the exact aspect. The orb, or
range of degrees, allowed between the
various planets in particular aspect in
order for that aspect to be effective
may range from just a few degrees to
as many as 17. Authorities differ

Orb (cont.)

widely on the effective orbs, but the closer the aspect, the more effective it's likely to be.

Outer Planets

Uranus, Neptune, and Pluto.

Part of Marriage

A formula derived from the positions of Ascendant, Descendant, and Venus. It is Ascendant + Descendant - Venus = the Part of Marriage. Its position in a chart will tell you something about marriage prospects and timing.

Part of Fortune

A formula derived from the positions of Ascendant, Moon, and Sun. The formula is Ascendant + Moon - Sun = Part of Fortune. Its position in a chart tells something about fortune in general, but also can be used in finding marriage times in the chart.

Part of Fascination

A formula derived from the positions of Ascendant, Venus, and Uranus. The formula is Ascendant + Venus - Uranus = Part of Fascination. When the Part of Fascination is found conjoining a significant planet or point in another's chart, there may be the type of fascination that could lead to marriage.

Part of Karma

A formula derived from the positions of Ascendant, Saturn, and Sun. The formula is Ascendant + Saturn - Sun = Part of Karma. Its position in a chart tells something about karma or connection from past lives between two people.

Pisces

See "Signs."

Planetary Ruler

The planet that rules each sign. See "Ruler."

Planetary Power

The effectiveness of a planet because of its favorable aspects, placement, or sign.

Planets

In astrology, the eight planets plus the luminaries, the Sun and the Moon, are all termed planets for convenience.

Sun — The Sun, as center of our solar system, symbolizes one's individuality as well as the male principle.

Moon — The Moon represents the emotions as well as the feminine principle.

Mercury — Mercury represents speech and communication as well as the type of mind.

Venus — Venus symbolizes love as well as beauty and represents the kind of woman a man favors.

Mars — Mars stands for passion and represents the kind of man a woman favors.

Jupiter — Jupiter is the planet of good fortune and abundance.

Saturn — Saturn represents age, experience, restrictions, and lack.

Uranus — Uranus symbolizes the unexpected and the unusual.

Neptune — Neptune is the planet of inspiration, fascination, mental telepathy, but also illusion and deceit.

Pluto — Pluto is the planet of power, transformation, and, as the ruler of Scorpio, sex, reproduction, and regeneration.

Pluto
See "Planets."

Progressed Planets
The positions of one's natal planets progressed forward to one's current age with one day in the ephemeris equaling one year of life. The aspects the progressed planets form when placed around your natal chart can show whether marriage or romance is likely during the current year.

Progressed Chart
A chart set up for the current year with one day in the ephemeris equal to one year of life. See "Progressed Planets."

Progressed Aspect
An aspect formed between progressed planets and natal planets or between progressed to progressed planets or progressed to converse planets.

Progressed Moon
The progressed Moon moves at the rate of approximately one degree per month and often indicates the month of marriage by its aspects.

Progressions
See "Progressed Planets."

Quincunx
See "Aspects."

Retrograde
The apparent backward motion of certain planets through the zodiac when viewed from the earth. Mercury is retrograde several times a year; Venus and Mars less often. People should be especially wary of Venus and Mars periods of retrograde motion when planning wed-dings or romantic engagements.

Rising Sign
The sign on the Ascendant or cusp of the first house.

Ruler, Rules, Ruled by
Each sign is said to have a ruler, which is associated with the meaning of that sign. Thus we say that Jupiter rules Sagittarius, or that Aries is ruled by Mars. The modern rulers of the twelve signs are:

Aries is ruled by Mars
Taurus is ruled by Venus
Gemini is ruled by Mercury
Cancer is ruled by the Moon
Leo is ruled by the Sun
Virgo is ruled by Mercury
Libra is ruled by Venus
Scorpio is ruled by Pluto
Sagittarius is ruled by Jupiter
Capricorn is ruled by Saturn
Aquarius is ruled by Uranus
Pisces is ruled by Neptune.

If Pisces is on the cusp of your tenth house, for instance, then Neptune, which rules Pisces, has an influence on tenth-house matters in your life.

Sagittarius
See "Signs."

Saturn
See "Planets."

Scorpio
See "Signs."

Secondary Directions
The most common method of progressing the natal chart. See "Progressed Planets."

Semisquare
A minor aspect. Half of a square or 45 degrees. See "Aspects."

Sesquisquare
A minor aspect. A square and a half or 135 degrees. See "Aspects." Also called "sesquiquadrate."

Sextile
A favorable aspect between planets in which two planets or points are sixty degrees apart. See "Aspects."

Signs
The twelve signs of the zodiac are:

Aries (March 21–April 19). A cardinal Fire sign ruled by Mars.

Taurus (April 20–May 20). A fixed Earth sign ruled by Venus.

Gemini (May 21–June 21). A mutable Air sign ruled by Mercury.

Cancer (June 22–July 22). A cardinal Water sign ruled by the Moon.

Leo (July 23–August 22). A fixed Fire sign ruled by the Sun.

Virgo (Aug. 23–Sept. 22). A mutable Earth sign ruled by Mercury.

Libra (Sept. 23–Oct. 22). A cardinal Air sign ruled by Venus.

Scorpio (Oct. 23–Nov. 21). A fixed Water sign ruled by Pluto.

Sagittarius (Nov. 22–Dec. 21). A mutable Fire sign ruled by Jupiter.

Capricorn (Dec. 22–Jan. 19). A cardinal Earth sign ruled by Saturn.

Aquarius (Jan. 20–Feb. 18). A fixed Air sign ruled by Uranus.

Pisces (Feb. 19–March 20) A mutable Water sign ruled by Neptune.

Solar Eclipse
See "Eclipse."

South Node
See "Lunar Nodes."

Square
A challenging major aspect in which two planets or points are ninety degrees apart. See "Aspects."

Sun Sign
The sign the Sun was moving through on the date of your birth. See "Zodiacal Order" or "Signs."

Sun/Moon Ties
The compatibility that results from a favorable aspect between one person's Sun and the other's Moon.

Sun
See "Planets."

Sun/Moon Midpoint
The zodiacal midpoint between the Sun and Moon in one's chart. Since these two are symbolic of the male and female energies, the point halfway between them is especially sensitive to transits and progressions and is often heavily aspected when marriage takes place. In addition, one can ascertain if a prospective partner is a probable partner through aspects in the other's chart to this midpoint.

T-Square
An astrological configuration formed by at least three planets or points in a chart. Two of these will be opposite each other, while a third will be square both. A T-square is thought to energize a person through the presence of obstacles or challenges.

Taurus
See "Signs."

Timer
See "Marriage Timer."

Transits
The passages of the planetary bodies in the heavens through the zodiac. As zodiacal degrees that aspect one's natal chart are transited by heavenly bodies, natal planets are activated, according to their natures and indications in the natal chart.

Trine
See "Aspects." The trine aspect is one of the most favorable. It indicates that planets or points are approximately 120 degrees apart in the zodiacal circle.

Triple-Wheel Computer Chart
A computer-produced chart that presents the natal chart in a center wheel, surrounded by two outer wheels of progressions and converse directions. With this drawn up for the current year, you can see if you have at least three to ten marriage aspects, an indicator of marriage possibilities.

Uranus
See "Planets."

Venus/Mars Ties
Favorable aspects between one person's Venus and a partner's Mars. Such ties are usually indicative of sexual attraction between male and female.

Venus
See "Planets."

Vertex
An additional chart angle. Conjunctions of a partner's planets to this angle may indicate a fated relationship.

Virgo
See "Signs."

Water Signs
Cancer, Scorpio, and Pisces. These are known as the emotional signs.

Zodiac Degree
The circle of the zodiac is divided into 360 degrees. Each degree is divided into 60 minutes. There are 30 degrees to each of the twelve signs of the zodiac wheel. Thus you might have a planet at 15 degrees of Aries (the first sign in the zodiac), which would mean that this planet is in the 15th degree of the zodiac. A planet at 15 degrees of Taurus (which is the second sign of the zodiac) would be in the 45th degree of the zodiac, etc.

Zodiacal Order
The order in which the signs follow each other in the zodiacal circle. This is Aries, Taurus, Gemini, Cancer, Leo, Virgo, Libra, Scorpio, Sagittarius, Capricorn, Aquarius, Pisces.

Bibliography

Arroyo, Steven. *Astrology, Psychology, and the Four Elements*. Reno, NV: CRCS Publications, 1975.

———. *Relationships & Life Cycles*. Reno, NV: CRCS Publications, 1979.

Ashmand, J. M. *Ptolemy's Tetrabiblos*. London: Foulsham & Co., Ltd., 1917.

Cross, Robert. *Raphael's Private Instructions in Genethliacal Astrology*. Chicago: The Aries Press, 1935.

Davison, Ronald C. *Synastry: Understanding Human Relations Through Astrology*. New York: ASI Publishers Inc., 1977.

———. *The Technique of Prediction*. London: L. N. Fowler & Co. Ltd., 1974.

Granite, Robert Hurzt. *The Fortunes of Astrology*. San Diego, CA: Astro Computing Services, 1980.

Grebner, Bernice Prill. *Lunar Nodes: New Concepts*. Tempe, AZ: American Federation of Astrologers, 1976.

Hand, Robert. *Planets in Transit*. Gloucester, MA: Para Research, Inc., 1976.

Leo, Alan. *A Thousand and One Notable Nativities*. Edinburgh: International Publishing Co., 1924.

McEvers, Joan. *Interpreting Your Sun-Ascendant*. Van Nuys, CA: Astro-Analytic Publications, 1970.

Moore, Marcia and Mark Douglas. *Astrology in Action*. York Harbor, Maine: Arcane Publications, 1970.

Parish, James Robert. *Hollywood's Great Love Teams*. New Rochelle, N.Y.: Arlington House Publishers, 1974.

Penfield, Marc. *An Astrological Who's Who*. York Harbor, Maine: Arcane Publications, 1972.

Rodden, Lois. *American Book of Charts*. San Diego, CA: Astro Computing Services, 1980.

——————. *Profiles of Women*. Tempe, AZ: American Federation of Astrologers, 1979.

Sargent, Lois Haines. *How to Handle Your Human Relations*. Washington, D.C.: American Federation of Astrologers, 1958.

Vaughan, Richard B. *Astrology in Modern Language*. Reno, NV: CRCS Publications, 1985.

Wright, Paul. *Astrology in Action*. Reno, NV: CRCS Publications, 1989.

Index

Air signs, 3–4, 6–8, 11, 16, 19, 26, 30, 40–41, 43, 185, 187, 198

Al-Biruni, 134

Albert, Prince, 98

alcoholic, 7, 34, 54

Allen, Woody, 138, 140, 154–155, 160

Anderson, Loni, 5

angles, 60, 66–69, 75, 77, 97–100, 107–111, 114, 118, 138, 149, 185–186, 190–191, 193

Arabic parts, 79, 112, 114, 133–135, 137, 139–143, 145, 147, 149, 186

Arroyo, Steven, 4

Ascendant, 8, 34, 52–53, 60, 66, 72–73, 75–76, 78, 89, 97–100, 102–103, 105, 110–111, 115, 118–120, 134–136, 138–140, 145–147, 149, 185–186, 189, 194–195, 197

aspect, 2, 7, 10, 16, 50–51, 54, 56–58, 64–66, 72–73, 76, 79, 82, 84–89, 91–93, 101–107, 109, 111, 117–120, 122, 125–129, 131, 137–138, 145–146, 148, 150, 186, 188, 192, 194, 196–199

Astaire, Fred, 3, 10, 103–104, 106

Astaire, Phyllis Potter, 3, 10, 103–104, 106

Astrology and the Four Elements, 4

Betty Ford Center, 37

Bouvier, Jacqueline, 6

Browning, Elizabeth Barrett, 10, 126–127, 130, 141, 153, 155, 161

Browning, Robert, 10, 126, 130, 141, 154, 162

Burton, Richard, 3, 11, 37, 50–51, 67–73, 76, 141, 154–155, 157–158

Charles, Prince of Wales, 74, 125, 141, 154–155, 163

Charles II, King, 8, 155, 164

Cleopatra, 37

Clinton, Bill, 5

Clinton, Hillary Rodham, 5

composite Sun/Moon midpoint, 122, 126–132, 187

computer services, 38

conjunction, 6, 11, 17, 30, 48–50, 57–58, 63–65, 68–70, 72, 82, 84, 97, 108–109, 115–116, 118, 122–123, 127–128, 138–140, 142–144, 146–148, 186–187, 190, 192, 194

converse directions, 50, 96–97, 100–101, 107–111, 113, 115–120, 127, 131, 145–150, 187–188, 196, 199

converse Ascendant, 111, 120

converse Descendant, 118, 120, 146, 149–150

converse IC, 100, 120, 131

converse Mars, 117, 146

converse Midheaven, 147

converse Moon, 111, 115–120, 148

converse Sun, 119–120, 127, 147, 150

converse Venus, 120, 146

Cross, Robert, 115

Davies, Marion, 9, 77, 85–87, 123, 141, 153, 155, 159

Davison, R.C., 97

decanates, 44–45, 188–189

Descendant, 52, 60, 66, 76, 97–100, 110–111, 118–120, 136, 138, 145–147, 149–150, 185–186, 189, 194

Diana, Princess of Wales, 74, 125, 134–135, 141, 153, 155, 165

difficult relationships, 65

duads, 44–45, 189

earning money, 82, 85

Earth signs, 9, 19, 30, 198

eastern horizon, 7, 66, 186, 189

eclipses, 59, 189–190, 198

Eddy, Nelson, 12, 154, 168

Edward VII, 13

eighth house, 42, 81, 83, 85–87, 89–90, 135, 141–142, 191

element, 3, 5–6, 8, 14, 37, 190

England, 8, 13, 98, 115, 154, 157–158, 161–165, 167, 174, 183

ephemeris, 47, 49, 52, 97, 100–101, 103–105, 107, 128, 187, 189–190, 196

ESP, 65

Farrow, Mia, 136–140, 153, 156, 169

fated relationship, 141, 200

fifth house, 18, 26, 36–37, 40, 44, 48–49, 51, 53, 55, 84, 86, 89, 98–99, 136, 139, 148, 191

Fire signs, 3–4, 6-7, 11, 16, 19, 26, 30, 39, 41–42, 137, 187, 189–190, 198

first house, 34, 36, 39–43, 53, 57, 86–87, 101, 106, 185–186, 189, 191, 197

Fisher, Eddie, 37

Fitzgerald, F. Scott, 7, 154, 156, 170

Fitzgerald, Zelda, 7, 153, 156, 171

fixed-sign squares, 5

Fortensky, Larry, 37, 97

free will, 97, 114

Gable, Clark, 2, 7, 128, 143, 154, 172

Garbo, 3

Gardner, Ava, 136, 153, 156, 173

Gifford, Frank, 6

Gilbert, 3

Grebner, Bernice Prill, 142

Griffith, Melanie, 6

Gwyn, Nell, 8, 141, 153, 174

hard aspect, 122, 127–128, 137

Hearst, William Randolph, 9, 77, 85, 123, 141, 154, 156, 159

Hearst Castle, 9, 123

Hilton, Nicky, 49

Hollywood, 3, 6–7, 103

Hollywood's Great Love Teams, 3

horoscope, 1, 3, 12–14, 38, 47, 49, 57, 82, 85, 87, 121, 185–187, 189–191, 193–194

house ruler, 34, 86, 90, 98–100, 104, 145, 191, 197

IC (see also Nadir), 60, 66, 68–69, 72, 75–77, 97–100, 108, 110–111, 117, 120, 131, 136, 138, 142–145, 147, 185, 191, 193

income, 82–83, 86, 90, 93

"iron butterfly" (see also "MacDonald, Jeanette"), 12

JFK, 6

Johnson, Don, 6

Jones, Marc Edmund, 139

Karma, 114, 134, 136–137, 140–145, 149–150, 195

karmic ties, 10, 14, 62, 64–66, 68, 79, 97, 133, 135, 137, 139–145, 147, 149, 192

Keats, John, 82–83

Kennedy, John Fitzgerald, 6, 127, 141, 154, 156, 175

Lee, Kathie, 6

Leigh, Vivien, 138

Lombard, Carole, 2, 7–8, 128, 143, 153, 156, 176

Louis XVI, King (of France), 88

love planets, 1, 3, 5, 7, 9, 11, 13–15, 17, 19, 21, 23, 25, 27, 29, 31, 35, 44, 47–59, 65, 73, 97–100, 107–108, 119, 192

Lovett, Lyle, 11, 16, 18

Loy, Mirna, 3, 6

lunar Nodes, 142, 192–194, 198

Lunar Nodes: New Concepts, 142

MacDonald, Jeanette, 12, 153, 156, 179

Madonna, 6, 102, 105

Marie Antoinette, 88, 153, 156, 178

marriage aspects, 95–96, 104–110, 113, 120, 148, 150, 193, 199

marriage indicators, 109, 121, 123, 125, 127, 129, 131

marriage partner, 13, 33, 35, 37, 39, 41, 43, 45, 189, 191

marriage timer, 111, 128, 145–146, 148–149, 193, 199

marriage year, 50, 97, 101, 107–108, 110–111, 145, 192

Mars, 1–2, 5-13, 17, 25–30, 34–35, 37–39, 44, 48–51, 56–57, 62–65, 67–79, 85–86, 89, 92, 96–100, 104–109, 111, 113, 116–117, 119–120, 131, 137, 144, 146–147, 150, 185, 188, 192–193, 195–198, 200

mate indicators, 43

MC (see also Midheaven), 60, 68–69, 72–73, 75–78, 98–100, 110–111, 145, 193

MGM film operettas, 12

Midheaven (see also MC), 60, 66, 82, 86, 97–100, 110, 136, 138, 141, 147, 149, 185, 193

midpoint, 79, 112, 121–132, 137–138, 187–188, 190, 193, 199

money luck, 9, 77, 81, 83–89, 91, 93

money planets, 82–85, 87–94, 191, 193

money rulers, 91

Monroe, Marilyn, 135

Moon, 1–2, 5-14, 34–35, 38–40, 44, 50, 53, 58–59, 62–63, 65–67, 69, 72–79, 83, 86–87, 89–92, 96–101, 104–105, 107–109, 111–132, 134–149, 186–187, 189–190, 192–199

Nadir (see also IC), 60, 66, 138, 193

negative degrees, 51

New Moon, 59, 109, 189, 194

Newman, Paul, 14, 122–123, 138, 141, 154, 156, 180

Node, 83, 87, 131, 141–142, 145, 148, 192–194, 198

North Node, 87, 131, 148, 192, 194

Olivier, Lawrence, 138

Onassis, Jaqueline Kennedy, 141, 154

Opposition, 5, 11–12, 34, 39–43, 52, 55–57, 63–65, 71–73, 83–84, 91, 111, 117, 122–123, 125, 128, 185–187, 191, 194

outer planets, 47–50, 52, 104–105, 128–129, 194

Parish, James Roberts, 3

Part of Fascination, 114, 134, 137, 139–140, 148–149, 195

Part of Fortune, 112, 114, 134–136, 143, 146–149, 194–195

Part of Karma, 114, 134, 137, 140–141, 143, 145, 149–150, 195

Part of Marriage, 97–99, 112, 114, 134, 136–139, 141, 145–146, 148, 194

partner indicator, 39–43

Penn, Sean, 6, 102, 105

possessions, 9, 82–83, 85, 87–88, 142, 191

Potter, Phyllis (Astaire), 3, 10, 103–104, 106

Powell, William, 3, 6

Prince of Wales, 154

Princess of Wales, 74, 153, 155, 165

progressed Ascendant, 147

progressed conjunction, 97

progressed Descendant, 146

progressed Mars, 116–117, 120, 150

progressed Midheaven, 147

progressed Moon, 104, 111–112, 114–116, 118–119, 196

progressed Sun, 100, 103, 127, 130, 150

progressed Venus, 119–120

progressions, 50, 57–58, 95–97, 101, 103–104, 107–109, 111, 145, 188, 196, 199

Ptolemy, 1, 6, 9, 12, 14

Quaid, Dennis, 18

quincunx, 91, 187, 193, 196

Raphael, 115

Reagan, Ronald, 116, 150

Restoration Period, 8

Reynolds, Burt, 5

rising sign, 34, 186, 189, 197

Roberts, Julia, 11, 16, 18

Rogers, Ginger, 10, 107

romance degrees, 50

Ryan, Meg, 18

San Simeon, 9, 123

Schwarzenneger, Arnold, 5, 18

second house, 39, 82–90, 191

Selleca, Connie, 13

semisquare, 82, 122, 125, 128–129, 187, 191, 193, 197

sesquiquadrate (see also sesquisquare), 127, 197

sesquisquare (see also sesquiquadrate), 122, 125–126, 128, 187, 191, 197

seventh house, 18–19, 34–38, 41, 44, 48–50, 53, 55, 78, 81, 96, 98–99, 101, 103–108, 110, 120, 142, 145, 148–149, 185, 189, 191, 193

sextile, 5, 10, 48–50, 52, 55, 57, 64, 70, 72, 75–76, 78, 103, 105–109, 120, 131, 137, 146–147, 186, 190–192, 197–198

sexual (physical) attraction, 2, 63, 65, 74, 76, 108, 137, 200

Shelley, Percy Bysshe, 99

Shriver, Maria, 5, 18

Simpson, Wallis (see also Duchess of Windsor), 13, 154, 166

Sinatra, Frank, 135, 137–138, 154, 181

Smith, Robyn, 104

Sonnets from the Portuguese, 10

South Node, 141–142, 145, 192, 198

squares, 5, 34, 51–53, 55, 65, 67, 71–73, 77–78, 84, 86, 90, 111, 123, 125

Sun, 1–17, 25-26, 35, 37–41, 44, 47–48, 50–51, 53, 57–59, 62–67, 69–79, 83–84, 86–87, 90–91, 96–101, 103–104, 106–109, 112–115, 117, 119–132, 134–141, 143–147, 149–150, 185–189, 192, 194–195, 197–199

Sun/Moon midpoint, 79, 112, 121–132, 137–138, 187, 199

Sun sign compatibility, 2–3

Taylor, Elizabeth, 11, 37, 48, 67, 97–98, 106, 154, 157–158

Tesh, John, 13

Tetrabiblos, 1

The Technique of Prediction, 97

Thin Man, 6

Todd, Mike, 11, 37, 50, 141, 154, 182

transits, 47–51, 53–59, 95, 111, 114, 128–130, 199

trine, 5–6, 8–11, 48–50, 52, 55, 57, 64, 70–72, 75–78, 82, 84, 86–90, 107–109, 116, 120, 137, 145–149, 186, 190–193, 199

triple-wheel, 107, 199

Venus, 1–2, 5–13, 17–26, 30, 35, 37–41, 48–51, 53, 57, 61–63, 65–69, 72–79, 82–84, 87–89, 92, 96–100, 104–105, 107–109, 111, 113, 116, 119–120, 130, 135–137, 139, 141, 143–147, 186, 192, 194–198, 200

Vertex, 141–143, 145, 200

Victoria, Queen, 98

Villiers, Barbara, 8, 154, 156, 183

Water signs, 3–4, 9, 11, 16–17, 19, 22, 28, 30, 37, 40, 42–43, 76, 116, 187, 198, 200

White House, 6

Windsor, Duke of, 13, 127, 141, 144, 149, 154, 156, 167

Windsor, Duchess of, 13, 127, 141–142, 144, 149, 154, 156, 166

Woodward, Joanne, 14, 122, 138, 141, 154, 184

Wyman, Jane, 116, 150

zodiac, 3, 17–19, 38, 44, 48–52, 56, 58, 114–115, 117, 120, 124, 127, 141, 185, 187–190, 192, 196, 198–200

On the following pages you will find listed, with their current prices, some of the books now available on related subjects. Your book dealer stocks most of these and will stock new titles in the Llewellyn series as they become available. We urge your patronage.

To Get a Free Catalog

You are invited to write for our bimonthly news magazine/catalog, *Llewellyn's New Worlds of Mind and Spirit*. A sample copy is free, and will continue coming to you at no cost as long as you are an active mail customer. You may subscribe for just $10 in the United States and Canada ($20 overseas, first class mail). Many bookstores also have *New Worlds* available—ask for it.

In *New Worlds* you will find news and features about new books, tapes, and services; announcements of meetings and seminars; helpful articles; and author interviews. Write to:

Llewellyn's New Worlds of Mind and Spirit
P.O. Box 64383-K479, St. Paul, MN 55164-0383, U.S.A.

To Order Books and Tapes

If your book store does not carry the titles described on the following pages, you may order them directly from Llewellyn by sending the full price in U.S. funds, plus postage and handling (see below).

Credit card orders: VISA, MasterCard, American Express are accepted. Call us toll-free within the U.S.A. and Canada at 1-800-THE-MOON.

Special Group Discount: Because there is a great deal of interest in group discussion and study of the subject matter of this book, we offer a 20% quantity discount to group leaders or agents. Our Special Quantity Price for a minimum order of five copies of *When Will You Marry?* is $51.80 cash-with-order. Include postage and handling charges noted below.

Postage and Handling: Include $4 postage and handling for orders $15 and under; $5 for orders over $15. There are no postage and handling charges for orders over $100. Postage and handling rates are subject to change. We ship UPS whenever possible within the continental United States; delivery is guaranteed. Please provide your street address as UPS does not deliver to P.O. boxes. Orders shipped to Alaska, Hawaii, Canada, Mexico and Puerto Rico will be sent via first class mail. Allow 4-6 weeks for delivery. International orders: Airmail – add retail price of each book and $5 for each non-book item (audiotapes, etc.); Surface mail – add $1 per item.
Minnesota residents add 7% sales tax.
Mail orders to:

Llewellyn Worldwide
P.O. Box 64383-K479
St. Paul, MN 55164-0383, U.S.A.

For customer service, call (612) 291-1970.

Computerized Astrology Reports

Simple Natal: Your chart calculated by computer in the Tropical/Placidus House system or the House system of your choice. It has all of the trimmings, including aspects, midpoints, Chiron and a glossary of symbols, plus a free booklet!
APS03-119. . . . . $5.00

Personality Profile Horoscope: Our most popular reading! This ten-part reading gives you a complete look at how the planets affect you. Learn about your general characteristics and life patterns. Look into your imagination and emotional needs. It is an excellent way to become acquainted with astrology and to learn about yourself. Very reasonable price!
APS03-503. . . . . $20.00

Transit Forecasts: These reports keep you abreast of positive trends and challenging periods. Transit Forecasts can be an invaluable aid for timing your actions and decision making. Reports begin the first day of the month you specify.
3-month Transit Forecast APS03-50 . . . . $12.00
6-month Transit Forecast APS03-501 . . . . $20.00
1-year Transit Forecast APS03-502. . . . . $25.00

Life Progressions: Discover what the future has in store for you! This incredible reading covers a year's time and is designed to complement the Personality Profile Reading. Progressions are a special system with which astrologers map how the "natal you" develops through specified periods of your present and future life, and with this report you can discover the "now you!"
APSO3-507 . . . . $20.00

Personal Relationship Reading: If you've just called it quits on one relationship and know you need to understand more about yourself before you test the waters again, then this is the report for you! This reading will tell you how you approach relationships in general, what kind of people you look for and what kind of people might rub you the wrong way. Important for anyone!
APS03-506. . . . . $20.00

Compatibility Profile: Find out if you really are compatible with your lover, spouse, friend or business partner! This is a great way of getting an in-depth look at your relationship with another person. Find out each person's approach to the relationship. Do you have the same goals? How well do you deal with arguments? Do you have the same values? This service includes planetary placements for both individuals, so send birth data for both and specify the type of relationship (i.e., friends, lovers, etc.). Order today!
APS03-504. . . . . $30.00

Ultimate Astro-Profile: This report has it all! Receive over 40 pages of fascinating, insightful and uncanny descriptions of your innermost qualities and talents. Read about your burn rate (thirst for change). Explore your personal patterns (from both the inside and outside). Examine the particular pattern of your Houses. The Astro-Profile doesn't repeat what you've already learned from other personality profiles, but considers the often neglected natal influence of the lunar nodes, plus much more!
APS03-505 . . . .$40.00

Computerized Charts for the Astrologer

Special offer!
Save $5! Order any *three* of these charts for just $25.
Save $10! Order any *five* for just $40.

Composite Chart: Save yourself hours of hand-calculating midpoints! This wheel combines the astrological data for both people into one chart to show how the blended energies work. This is a particularly good chart for an already existing long-term relationship like a marriage.
APS03-520 . . . .$10.00

Relationship Chart: Check the transits to this chart for significant times in a couple's life. This wheel plots the midpoints between the partners' birth time and location.
APS03-521 . . . .$10.00

Bi-Wheel Chart: Learn how you perceive one another. The first wheel plots your partner's natal chart outside your chart, and the second wheel plots your chart outside your partner's. Comes with synastry table: an at-a-glance grid that shows all the aspects between two people.
APS03-522 . . . .$10.00

Solar Return Chart: Every year, around your birthday, the Sun returns to the same point in your chart where it was at your birth. It is an important point as it begins a new cycle for the coming year. This chart sets the stage for the influences and experiences of the next 12 months and is a valuable forecasting tool.
APS03-523 . . . .$10.00

Electional Chart: Have you set a wedding date? The electional chart shows you whether the date you have chosen to begin (or end) a venture—be it a marriage, business partnership, or major purchase—will get you off on the right foot or foreshadow bleak times.
APS03-524 . . . .$10.00

Marriage Year Chart: This is the Triple Wheel Chart described in chapter seven of When Will You Marry? (It provides your natal chart in the inner circle, secondary directions in the middle circle, and converse directions in the outside wheel.) Follow Rose Murray's simple instructions on page 107 to determine whether the year in question is (or was!) your best year for marriage. Be sure to indicate the year for which you want the chart cast.
APS03-519 . . . .$10.00

HOW TO ORDER ASTROLOGICAL CHARTS

(1) fill out this order form.
(2) Use birth certificate for accurate information.
(3) Send order by mail. **No phone orders, please.**
Use additional sheet of paper if necessary.

Name of Service	Order #APS03-	Price
_____	_____	_____
_____	_____	_____
_____	_____	_____
_____	_____	_____
_____	_____	_____
_____	_____	_____
_____	_____	_____
	TOTAL	_____

FIRST PERSON

_____
FULL NAME
Mam Mpm

_____
BIRTH TIME   DATE   YEAR

_____
BIRTHPLACE – CITY, COUNTY, STATE, COUNTRY

SECOND PERSON

_____
FULL NAME
Mam Mpm

_____
BIRTH TIME   DATE   YEAR

_____
BIRTHPLACE – CITY, COUNTY, STATE, COUNTRY

_____
DATE OF EVENT (for Electional or Marriage Year Charts)

BILLING INFORMATION

_____
NAME

_____
ADDRESS

_____
CITY   STATE   ZIP

_____
DAYTIME PHONE (if we have questions)

Make checks or money orders payable to
Llewellyn Worldwide.

CHARGE IT!

M VISA   M MasterCard   M Am Express

_____
CARD NUMBER   EXP. DATE

_____
SIGNATURE OF CARDHOLDER

MAIL THIS FORM WITH PAYMENT TO
Llewellyn Astrological Services
P.O. Box 64383-479, St. Paul, MN 55164-0383

Please allow 4-6 weeks for delivery
Thank you for your order!

For Readers of
When Will You Marry?

Save 30% on your Compatibility Profile! Now just $21

Thank you for purchasing *When Will You Marry?* Now you can save 30% on your compatibility chart (regularly priced at $30). Find out if you really are compatible with your lover, spouse, friend, or business partner! Find out each person's approach to the relationship. Do you have the same values? How well do you deal with conflict? Since this profile includes planetary placements for both individuals, send birth data for both and specify the type of relationship (i.e., friends, lovers, etc.). Order #APSO3-504

Do not photocopy this form. Only this original will be accepted.
Check your birth certificate for the most accurate information

FIRST PERSON

FULL NAME
_____
• am • pm
BIRTH TIME   DATE   YEAR

BIRTHPLACE – CITY, COUNTY, STATE, COUNTRY

SECOND PERSON

FULL NAME
_____
• am • pm
BIRTH TIME   DATE   YEAR

BIRTHPLACE – CITY, COUNTY, STATE, COUNTRY

MAIL THIS FORM WITH PAYMENT TO
Llewellyn Astrological Services
P.O. Box 64383-479, St. Paul, MN 55164-0383

Please allow 4-6 weeks for delivery.
Thank you for your order!

BILLING INFORMATION

NAME
_____
ADDRESS
_____
CITY   STATE   ZIP
_____
DAYTIME PHONE

Make checks or money orders payable to Llewellyn Worldwide.

CHARGE IT!

• VISA   • MasterCard   • Am Express

CARD NUMBER   EXP. DATE
_____
SIGNATURE OF CARDHOLDER

The Book of Lovers
Men Who Excite Women, Women Who Excite Men
by Carolyn Reynolds

What are you looking for in a lover or potential mate? If it's money, set your sights on a Pisces/ Taurus. Is health food your passion? Then a Virgo/Cancer will share it with you.

In *The Book of Lovers*, astrologer Carolyn Reynolds introduces a new way to determine romantic compatibility through the use of Sun and Moon sign combinations. Best of all, you don't have to know a thing about astrology to use this book!

You will find descriptions of every man and woman born between the years 1900 and 2000. To see whether that certain someone could be "the one," simply locate his or her birthdata in the chart and flip to the relevant pages to read about your person's strengths and weaknesses, sex appeal, personality, and, most importantly, how they will treat you!

0-87542-289-0, 464 pgs., 6 x 9, softcover $14.95

Heaven Knows What
by Grant Lewi

What better way to begin the study of astrology than to actually do it while you learn. *Heaven Knows What* contains everything you need to cast and interpret complete natal charts without memorizing any symbols, without confusing calculations, and without previous experience or training. The tear-out horoscope blanks and "aspect wheel" make it easy.

The author explains the influence of every natal Sun and Moon combination, and describes the effects of every major planetary aspect. His readable and witty interpretations are so relevant that even long-practicing astrologers gain new insight into characteristics of the signs and meanings of the aspects.

Grant Lewi is sometimes called the father of "do-it-yourself" astrology, and is considered by many to have been astrology's forerunner to the computer.

0-87542-444-9, 372 pgs., 6 x 9, tables, charts, softcover. $12.95

The Instant Horoscope Reader
Planets by Sign, House and Aspect
by Julia Lupton Skalka

Find out what was written in the planets at your birth! What does it mean to have Gemini on your 8th house cusp? What does it mean if your Sun is conjoined with natal Jupiter?

The Instant Horoscope Reader was written to answer such questions. You will find the meaning of the placement of the Sun, Moon and each planet, including aspects between the natal planets, the meaning of the houses in the horoscope and house rulerships. Even if you have not had your chart cast, this book includes simple tables that enable you to locate approximate placements and aspects for unique perspectives about yourself and others.

ISBN: 1-56718-669-6, 6 x 9, 272 pp., illus $14.95

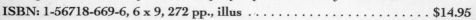